NO MORE BAD DATES

High Tea

KATE O'KEEFFE

Wild Lime Books

Wild Lime
Books

Edited by The Letterers Collective
Copyright © 2019 Kate O'Keeffe

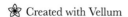 Created with Vellum

About This Book

Three friends form the No More Bad Dates Pact: stop dating the wrong guys and start dating the right ones - weirdos and jerks need not apply.

Twenty-five-year-old Sophie McCarthy's career is virtually nonexistent, her family expects her to "do something important" with her life, and she's totally sick of dating the wrong guys: the self-absorbed, the arrogant, the borderline criminally insane.

After she's unceremoniously dumped during the vows at her boss's wedding, she and her two equally disappointed-in-love best friends agree to help each other find decent guys to date. Together, they form the No More Bad Dates Pact: stop dating the wrong guys and start dating the right ones--weirdos and jerks need not apply.

When Sophie's roommate Jason Christie--a.k.a. doctor-in-training and serial nurse-dater--joins the pact, he vows to weed out the bad ones for her. But with his rejection of every guy Sophie meets, she begins to wonder if he's got an ulterior motive. And anyway, why does she always have so much more fun with Jason than with the guys she's actually trying to date?

While desperately seeking her "happy for now," could Sophie stumble into her "happily ever after?"

Also by Kate O'Keeffe

It's Complicated Series:

Never Fall for Your Back-Up Guy

Never Fall for Your Enemy

Love Manor Romantic Comedy Series:

Dating Mr. Darcy

Marrying Mr. Darcy

Falling for Another Darcy

Falling for Mr. Bingley (spin-off novella)

High Tea Series:

No More Bad Dates

No More Terrible Dates

No More Horrible Dates

Cozy Cottage Café Series:

One Last First Date

Two Last First Dates

Three Last First Dates

Four Last First Dates

Wellywood Romantic Comedy Series:

Styling Wellywood

Miss Perfect Meets Her Match

Falling for Grace

Standalone titles

Manhattan Cinderella

The Right Guy

One Way Ticket

Prologue

Two Months Ago

I love weddings. The emotion, the vows, the optimism, the dress. All of it. I know I'm a total romantic, and about a gazillion marriages end in divorce every year, but I don't care. When I watch a happy couple show the world their love, tears well in my eyes and my heart expands because in that moment, something utterly magical happens.

What more can I say? I love weddings, pure and simple.

Or at least I did until *the thing* happened.

Picture this. I'm at a beautiful, emotional, swept-up-in-it-all type of wedding. I'm sitting on an uncomfortably hard wooden pew, the scent in the air a heady mixture of flowers and polished wood. The late-afternoon light filters through the ornate stained glass windows, illuminating the beautiful bride and her handsome groom.

So far, so wonderful.

As I watch the bride, dressed in the most beautiful vintage fifties wedding dress I've seen—nipped in at the waist, showing off all her curves to (classy) perfection—her Norse god-like husband-to-be reaches out and takes her hands in his. They gaze at one another, their faces alight with a love so real, I can almost reach out and touch it.

Which I don't, of course. That would be weird.

Instead, I turn and smile at my boyfriend, my hand over my heart. Andrew glances at me briefly before he returns his attention to the vows.

"Bailey. I love you more than I could ever imagine loving anyone. You are my life, my soul. Reflected in your eyes, I am a better man. Thank you." Ryan's voice, a.k.a. the voice of Thor, the Norse god, cracks with emotion, and half the congregation—*all* the women and probably most of the men, although I bet they would never admit it—reach for their tissues.

I open my clutch and pull out a Kleenex. I dab at my eyes and glance once more at Andrew. Noticing his brows knitted together, I smile, embarrassed. "What Ryan said?" I whisper, my voice trembling. "So, so perfect."

"Yeah, it was all right, I guess. If you go in for that sort of crap," Andrew replies, crinkling his nose with distaste.

Crap? What does he mean, *crap?*

I open my mouth to ask, but now isn't the time. Bailey has begun her own vows, her voice so heavy with emotion, I'm amazed any of us can make out a single word. I think she's saying something about Ryan being her best friend, and how he's helped her become the vermin she is. No, wait. That would be how he's helped her become the *woman* she is. Yes, that sounds much more appropriate and wedding-y.

The problem is, I'm so busy trying to work out what's going on with my boyfriend, I've lost all focus on the ceremony unfolding before my eyes. Sure, I know he's not the most romantic of souls, but even a rugby-playing, one-of-the-guys, rugged type like Andrew can see how much these two love each other, right? I mean, he's not a freaking robot.

I nudge him in the ribs. "You okay?"

"Yup. Fine." His words are clipped, and he keeps his eyes trained on the couple at the altar.

And then it hits me. I know what's going on here! He's being swept away by the beauty of it all, too, only he wants to appear all manly and stoic. He's *pretending* to be grumpy to cover it up. Guys pull dumb stuff like that all the time. I should know; I've dated a few.

A few too many, actually.

I lean closer to him and place my hand on his. "I think it's wonderful. They love each other so much."

Andrew harrumphs in response.

I pat his hand knowingly. "It's okay, honey. I know you feel it, too." I settle back into my seat, prepared once more to be tangled up in the love emanating from the soon-to-be-wed couple, when I notice a girl in the aisle opposite us turn and smile. She's wearing an eye-catching red dress that leaves little to the imagination. It's totally inappropriate for a wedding, in my opinion, but she's rocking it, that's for sure. I smile back at her and wonder how I know her. Maybe she's a customer at the Cozy Cottage Café? I've worked there for a few years now, and I often see our regulars out and about in the city.

Her face flushes and she looks away.

Weird.

And then it happens again.

"Who's she?" I whisper to Andrew.

"Who?"

"The girl in the red dress. She keeps smiling at me, and I can't think who she is."

"Oh, err . . . Cindy, I think? Or Sandy? Something like that. We met her at that karaoke bar you love so much," Andrew replies.

"Jojo's? Really? I don't remember." I give his hand another squeeze and return my attention to the wedding.

"—the power invested in me, I now pronounce you husband and wife," the priest exclaims. "You may kiss!"

As Bailey and Ryan do precisely that, the congregation erupts into applause. Swept up in the sheer romance of the moment, I go out on a limb. Not because I'm "there" with Andrew yet exactly, more because, well, we could be. Some day. I put my hand on his arm and whisper, "Who knows? Maybe, one day, we'll fall in love like them?"

He whips his head in my direction, and I pull back in shock. "We'll do what?"

Less sure now, I reply, "Fall in love . . .?"

Yeah, I'm persisting with the lunacy. What can I do? I'm committed. I need to follow through. But really, is it such an outrageous idea my boyfriend could fall in love with me?

"Some day?" His brows knit together, almost forming a perfect mono-brow. It's not a great look, I've got to say.

"Well, not now. *Obviously*," I say hastily in a weak attempt to backtrack. "We've only been dating for a couple of months. But some day. You know, in the future." When all he does is gawp at me, those brows of his threatening to meet permanently in the middle, I add, "In the distant future, far, far away, when little green men rule the Earth and we have robots to do the dishes."

Little green men? Robots? *Dishes?* What the heck am I talking about?

Saving me from my nervous ramblings, the organ bursts to life as beaming newlyweds Bailey and Ryan begin their happy walk, hand-in-hand back down the aisle. As they make their way past us, I smile and wave—and try to forget how I put myself out there in a thoroughly humiliating way a couple of moments ago.

As I step toward the end of the aisle, I feel Andrew's hand on my arm, and I turn back to look at him.

"Okay, here's the thing," he begins.

He's going to explain his weirdness from before. Perhaps he's going to open up to me? Tell me how he feels? Tell me that he too thinks that one day we might fall in love, maybe even get married?

"Ok*aaay*," I lead, doing my best to suppress an expectant smile.

"We've had a good ride, right?"

Well. I wasn't expecting that. Puzzled, I ask, "A good ride?"

"Yeah, you know. You and me, dating. Whatever."

I smile to myself. Whoever said rugby players were inarticulate thugs clearly hasn't met Andrew Foster. I place my hand on his big, muscular arm (dating a rugby player has got its benefits, too).

"We're great. And I won't go mentioning love again. Not for a while, anyway. It was a heat of the moment thing with Bailey and Ryan looking so perfect up there, nothing more."

"No, what I mean is it was a good ride. You and me, Sophie. We've had fun, but . . . it's over." He looks down at his shoes.

Wait, what?

I blink at him, trying to work out if he's saying what I think he's saying. "It's over? What's over?"

"Us. You and me. Sorry about that." His gaze drops down to his shoes once more, which have evidently become quite fascinating in the last few seconds.

I hit the internal panic button. "You're breaking up with me?" I say a little too loudly. Several members of the congregation turn their heads to look at me. "You're-you're breaking up with me?" I say at a less hysterical, but nonetheless totally freaked-out volume.

Because, seriously? *Here?*

He shrugs. "Yeah, I guess."

I shake my head, the neurons in my brain sparking in a million different directions at once.

How?

Why?

What?!!

"You're breaking up with me at my *boss's wedding?*"

His lips form a grim line. "Yup."

"But-but why?" I manage, my throat so dry I'm not sure I'll ever be able to swallow again.

He looks up again and shrugs. "I dunno. It's not working, I guess. Look, Sophie, I didn't mean to do this now, you know? But it kinda came up with the thing you said about us falling in love some-day." He pulls a face to show me exactly how distasteful that notion is to him. "I decided I should, you know, rip off the Band-Aid."

My heart thrashes against my chest as though it's trying to escape through my ribs. "So, this is it? We're over?"

He twists his mouth and nods.

Stunned, I turn away from him and gaze blindly around the church as people begin to follow the newlyweds outside. The organ still blares as people around us chat and laugh as though nothing has happened.

My eyes settle on my other boss, Paige. She's got her arms wrapped around her husband's arm as they move slowly with the congregation out of the church. She shoots me a happy grin, and I try to smile back. It doesn't work.

I shuffle closer to the edge of our row and blindly follow everyone outside. Andrew must be behind me, but I don't look back. Once out of the church, I take a deep, gulping breath as I blink in the brilliant sunshine.

I feel a hot hand on my shoulder and look up. "I guess I'll, ah, see you 'round, Sophie," Andrew murmurs.

"Uh" is all I can manage in my zombie-like state.

He turns and begins to weave his way through the guests. I blink then watch him leave until all I can see is the back of his head.

Blindsided. Yup, I know exactly how that word feels now. And it is not a nice feeling.

Sure, Andrew and I have only been dating two months, give or take. I know that's not a long time in the scheme of things, but for me, well, it's close to a record. James Chisholm lasted three months and four and a half days back in high school, and me and all my friends were convinced we would be together forever.

Andrew was . . . what was he? My perfect guy? Ah, no. The man I want to spend the rest of my life with? The man I want to grow old with? Definitely not, despite my recent "swept up in the moment," totally ill-advised comments.

I'm not going to do *that* again in a hurry.

I guess the best thing about Andrew was he was mine, imperfections and all. And now I've got no one, alone at my boss's wedding, dumped and dazed.

This is so not the way I expected today to go when I woke up this morning. I thought I'd watch my lovely boss marry her Thor-like man, probably shed a tear or two at the sheer romance of the day, have a glass or two of wine, and dance with my boyfriend.

Not get dumped mere moments after the happy couple says, "I do."

"Hi, Sophie. You look gorgeous today."

Still in a freshly-dumped fog, I try to focus on who's talking to me. It's Cassie, one of the Cozy Cottage Café regulars and one of Bailey's BFFs. "Hey, Cassie." I force a bright smile. If it looks even half as unconvincing as it feels, she doesn't comment.

"Stunning wedding, right? Bailey looks so, so beautiful. I knew she would."

I look over at the bride. She looks almost luminous in the bright summer afternoon sun. "She does."

A red dress behind Bailey grabs my attention, and it takes me a few seconds for the scene unfolding in front of me to register. Is that . . . ? Is she with . . .? My brain refuses to comprehend what's staring me in the face. I scrunch my eyes shut and ping them open again.

"Are you okay?" Cassie's voice sounds like it's coming from the other end of a long tunnel.

"I'm fine," I mumble as I stare, now completely fixated by the scene in front of me.

"No, you're not." Cassie must follow my line of vision, because she adds, "Isn't that the guy you came with?"

I swallow, my throat suddenly dry as I watch Andrew and the girl in the red dress together. Cindy or Sandy. Whatever he said her name is, she's all over him, simpering and giggling and generally carrying on as though he were her favorite flavor of ice cream.

I blink again, my insides twisting. Unceremoniously dumped and publicly humiliated, all within ten minutes flat.

This has got to be the worst date of my life.

Chapter 1

Present Day

As the last note leaves my lips, I know the room heaves a collective sigh of relief.

Despite my aspirations to be New Zealand's answer to Lady Gaga, I know I'm not what anyone would call a great singer. Or even a good singer. At best, I'm passable. Although judging by the looks on my friends' faces when I get back to our table, I didn't quite reach the lofty heights of "passable" tonight.

Just another one of my failings.

"Great job, babe," Darcy says with a pat on my back as I sit down at our table.

"Oh, yeah. Great job. You were super good, tonight, Soph," Erin echoes.

I look from one grinning, over-eager face to the other. Erin and Darcy are the best friends a girl could have, but when it comes to me, honesty is not exactly their strong point right now.

I press my lips together as laughter begins to bubble up inside me. It's no use. In seconds, I'm doubled over, and after a beat, my friends join in.

"Oh, my God. I was terrible up there," I manage between giggles.

I know neither Darcy nor Erin will come out and actually say it. Since the day Andrew dumped me at Bailey's wedding and went off with the next girl, they've been walking on tiny, precious eggshells around me. Apparently, I've never looked better, I'm the best barista in the Southern Hemisphere, and the world has been starved of my musical prowess for far too long.

None of that is true, of course, especially the musical prowess thing.

"You weren't terrible, Soph." Erin shakes her head as she wipes the tears of laughter from under her eyes. "You got the melody right. Well, some of the time, anyway."

"And you looked super cute in that new dress up there," Darcy adds and she and Erin both nod. "Only, maybe next time, babe, why don't you *not* choose a Kelly Clarkson song?"

"It's my anthem. Kelly's my soul sister," I protest. "I love 'Stronger!'"

"Honey, it doesn't love you," Darcy says in a rare moment of honesty, winning a slap on the arm from Erin. "Ouch!"

Erin glares at Darcy. "This is for fun, and it's good therapy for Soph."

I let out a puff of air. "You girls are great. I sucked. I know it, you know it, everyone here knows it. Watch this." I lean back in my chair and tap a guy on the shoulder behind me. "Excuse me, sir. Did you like the way I sang that song a minute ago?"

His eyes dart from me to my friends and back again. "Uh, I don't know what to say."

"Be honest. I sucked, right?"

He chortles. "Howler monkeys have nothing on you. I mean, that top note? Ouch! And then in the chorus when you tried to hold—"

I've heard more than enough, I cut him off. "Yes, okay. I got it. Thank you." Some people don't know how to sugar-coat things, do they? I turn back to my friends. "See?"

"A howler monkey? He could have been nicer about it," Erin complains.

"You chose that song because you're feeling stronger, right?" Darcy asks hopefully. "It's time you got over that jerk, Soph. Andrew Foster is not worth your time."

"Totally," Erin agrees. "The way he dumped you at that wedding and then hooked up with that girl? Jerk."

"Scum."

"A-hole."

It's like watching a game of tennis between these two, the ball being insults to label my ex.

"I know." I let out a puff of air and slump my shoulders. "I heard they're still dating, him and the red-dress wedding hook-up girl." I try to keep the bitterness from my voice. Fail. "I mean, who wears a scarlet red dress with a plunging neckline to a wedding? So inappropriate."

"Babe, we've been talking, and we think it's time you moved on," Darcy says as Erin nods. "I mean, look around you. There are cute men everywhere." She gestures around the room.

I follow where she's pointing to a table of middle-aged men. Their hair is thinning, their beer bellies are pressed up against the table, and at least one of them looks old enough to be my dad. "Those guys? I may be dateless, but I'm not desperate. Not yet, anyway."

"I don't mean them, specifically. I just mean there are lots of guys out there, that's all." Darcy has that stern look on her face, the one I bet she uses to get things done in her job as personal assistant to a local celebrity. "You're twenty-five. Enough with the moping. It's time to get out and get amongst it."

I shake my head. "The problem is, I think I suck at choosing who to date."

"No, you don't," Erin protests.

"Yes, I do. Need I remind you of Andrew?"

"She's right. She does." Darcy presses her lips together as she nods. "And I'm not just talking about Andrew Foster. Remember that guy you dated last year? What was his name? The one with the tropical fish your cat ate."

"Kyle Butler." The way he dumped me over that darn fish still stings. Talk about an overreaction. "In her defense, Freckles is a born hunter. She can't help it. It's her instinct. And anyway, I really didn't think he'd notice."

"I don't get what your cat was doing at his apartment in the first place," Erin says.

"I brought her to keep me company when I went to feed his stupid fish. He was out of town, and I was only trying to help him out."

Darcy snaps her fingers. "Focus, girls. Look at that guy over there." She points at a guy in a navy shirt and jeans, leaning against the bar. "He's really cute. Just your type, Soph."

I size him up. He's probably about our age, maybe a few years older. He's good looking, that's for sure, but with his blond hair and fair skin, he could almost be related to me.

"How do I know he's not a jerk? How do I know he won't dump me at a wedding, or freak out over some fish? Which, by the way, wasn't even that nice to look at. Why Freckles chose that one to kill and not one of the other more beautiful ones, I just don't know."

"She's right, Darcy," Erin says. "We're all single. We've all had our fair share of bad dates and bad relationships. All we want is to date nice, decent guys, right?" Darcy and I both nod. "This isn't just about Sophie. It's about all of us."

Darcy's shoulders slump. "Yeah. I guess it is."

"See? It's a hopeless situation," I say. "We may as well agree to stay single the rest of our lives. It's a whole lot easier. And it'd cost a lot less in replacement fish."

"How much was it?" asks Erin.

"$350."

"What?" Erin does her best impersonation of fish eyes. "$350 for a fish you don't even eat?"

"Freckles did," Darcy says with a sardonic smile. "So, what are we going to do about it?"

I push my eyebrows together. "The dead fish?"

Darcy shakes her head. "No, not the dead fish. What are we going to do about the fact we keep on dating the wrong guys?"

A seed of an idea begins to grow in my mind. "My bosses agreed to a dating pact."

Darcy sucks her cocktail up through a straw and asks, "What sort of dating pact?"

"They called it the 'Last First Date Pact.' Basically, they agreed that the next guy they each dated would be The One," I explain.

Darcy's eyes get huge. "Geez Louise! The pressure! Can you imagine?"

"So, if you go on a date with a guy, whether you like him or not, you're stuck with him. Like, *forever*?" Erin asks.

"Yup. Although they did vet the guys first."

"That sounds like its own special kind of crazy, right there," Darcy says.

"I hear you. It sounds insane. But let me tell you something that might change your mind. Of the four friends who went in on the pact, three are married, and the other one is so loved-up with her guy, it makes me feel like breaking something every time they're in the café together. Well, since Andrewgate, anyway."

Erin's eyebrows ping up to meet her hairline. "Are you saying the pact worked out for every single one of them?"

I nod. "Mm-hm."

Erin puts her hands in the air. "Okay. You got me."

"Me too. How does it work?" Darcy asks.

"I don't know, exactly. All I know is they agreed that they weren't going to date anyone who didn't have the potential to be their H.E.A." I lift my cocktail to my lips and take a sip.

"H.E.A.?" Darcy questions.

"Happily Ever After, babe," Erin explains. "You should read romance novels rather than those thrillers you like so much. Most of them end with a wonderful, satisfying H.E.A."

"Sounds too predictable to me," Darcy scoffs.

"They are predictable, but no one cares. Because they're wonderful." Erin grins, her hand on her heart.

"Maybe the three of us could agree to some sort of pact?" I suggest.

Darcy pushes her long dark hair behind her ear. "It seems super serious to me."

"Yeah, and super scary," Erin adds. "I'm not even sure I want to get married yet. I just want to date nice guys. Ones that won't steal my shoes."

Darcy laughs. "OMG, I totally forgot that happened to you!"

"What do you think he did with them?" I ask. "He couldn't have worn them. You've got feet the size of a seven-year-old."

"Hey! I may be short, but I'm perfectly formed," Erin protests. "At least that's what Dad always tells me. And I do not want to think about what Mark did with my shoes." She shivers. "What a creep."

"Guys with weird shoe fetishes aside, I'm with you, girl. I'm not in the marriage space either, not like my sisters. *Boring*," Darcy says. "Dating is fun. But I would love to date some nice guys for a change."

"That's called an H.F.N., Darce: Happy For Now," Erin explains helpfully.

"Where do you get all these acronyms, Erin?" Darcy asks.

"I told you, romance novels. Although I much prefer an H.E.A. to an H.F.N."

Darcy puts her head in her hands. "Stop hurting my brain, Erin."

I try the expression out. "Happy For Now. I like the sound of that. Nothing too serious, nothing too permanent. Just . . . happy for now."

Erin nods. "Exactly."

Darcy looks back up at us. "Happy is good, and the 'for now' part sounds a whole lot less scary than 'forever,' that's for sure."

I tap my chin as I formulate an idea. "Girls? How about we make a pact that we're only going to date the good guys. No more jerks, no more creeps with weird shoe fetishes," I raise my eyebrows at Erin, "no weirdos obsessed with sea life, and definitely no more jerks who dump us at weddings."

A flicker of a smile spreads across Darcy's face. "The No More Bad Dates Pact."

Erin nods, Darcy's smile catching. "The No More Bad Dates Pact. I like it. OMG, we could hashtag it! It'll become a thing, like Jimmy Fallon's worst first dates from a while back. It could be so fun!"

"I'm not interested in trending. I'm interested in dating non-jerks, and having some fun," I say.

"We could do both?" Erin suggests with a hopeful look on her gorgeous face. "#NoMoreBadDates."

"Of course we can!" Darcy's excitement matching mine.

I beam at both my friends. "Hashtag or no hashtag, we're agreed. We're going to date nice guys, guys we want to be with, guys who actually *deserve* us."

"Yes!" they both reply with gusto.

I raise my glass, and my friends follow suit. "To the No More Bad Dates Pact. May it bring us all our H.F.N.s."

As we clink glasses, I feel a rush of optimism for the first time since that fateful day with Andrew. The No More Bad Dates Pact sounds like exactly what I need. I cannot wait to start.

Chapter 2

I close the door to my apartment as quietly as I can manage. I don't want to rouse my roommate from sleep. It's after one in the morning, and he works crazy hours as a trainee doctor. I like to think of myself as a considerate roommate, after all.

I slip off my heels and pad lightly across the hardwood floors of the hallway toward the kitchen. After all that karaoke singing and plotting the No More Bad Dates Pact, I need a glass of water. As I near the kitchen, I hear a distinctly female giggle coming from the adjacent living room. Hmm. Jason must be "entertaining." I'll grab a glass of water and head straight to bed. I drop my clutch onto the kitchen counter and open the top cupboard to pull out a glass as something furry and purring brushes up against my legs.

"Hello, Freckles." I pick my cat up and give her a cuddle. She's warm and fluffy, and her purr grows to almost jackhammer proportions as I scratch her head. "I was talking about you tonight. Have you had a good evening? Did you do some fun cat things like sleep or purr or clean yourself?"

Her response is to close her eyes, her cat motor running, and look about as blissed-out as any creature can get.

Oh, to be a cat. I smile. "I'll take that as a yes, then, shall I, Freckles?"

I place her back on the floor and pour her a small bowl of milk, which she laps up. Literally. I walk over to the sink and fill my glass with water, and then lean back against the counter and watch her. She's content in her little world, always happy to see me and curl up beside me when I sleep. For Freckles, life is uncomplicated, straight-forward, and happy. She gets up, does cat things, sleeps, does more cat things, and then sleeps some more. Easy. "I bet you don't have to make a pact to date non-jerks," I murmur.

"You talking to yourself again, McCarthy?" Seemingly out of thin air, Jason appears at my side, making me almost drop the glass in my hand. "I could get you assessed, you know, see what madness lurks beneath."

"Don't creep up on me like that, dude," I protest.

"You were too busy either talking to yourself or your fur ball cat. *Dude.*"

"She's not a fur ball. She happens to be feline aristocracy," I quip.

Okay, I'm making this up as I go, but Jason deserves it right now. Roommates should sign an agreement that they'll keep out of one another's business—even if I quite like having him around.

His laugh is low and soft. "Did you have a good night? Your regular karaoke gig with the girls, right?"

"Yup."

"How were the vocals tonight? On point?"

"Naturally. Well, as 'on point' as I can be. Darcy sang that new song you hear everywhere right now, and she sounded great. Erin did an ABBA song, as she always does." I roll my eyes. Erin refuses to move her musical taste into this century. It's like she got stuck listening to her parents' music when she was little and never managed to shake it off. "Then the three of us sang 'Bohemian Rhapsody' at the end, which was so fun, although I'm sure I saw some guy in the audience doing the sign of the cross."

There's a glint in his eye when he asks, "Because you were so good?"

"Yeah, Jas. Because I was so good." I collect my purse from the counter. "Who've you got here?"

"One of the nurses from the hospital."

I shake my head. "Doctors and nurses, huh? A combination as cliché as—"

When I don't offer anything further, Jason says, "As cliché as what?"

I shrug. "As doctors and nurses. You're so cliché, there are soap operas about you guys."

He shakes his head. "It's meant to be, I guess."

"Shouldn't you be getting back to your nurse, Mr. Stereotype?"

"She just left."

"She did?" I look down the hallway to the front door. "How did I miss that?"

"It may shock you, but I do things you don't know about sometimes."

I put my hand over my heart. "That is truly, truly shocking. Why have you never told me this before?"

"It's on a need-to-know basis." He pushes himself effortlessly and perches on the counter. "So, any gossip from the girls' night?"

"Of course. There's always gossip. It wouldn't be a girls' night if there wasn't."

"And?" he prods.

I place my glass on the counter and lean up against it. "And we made a group decision on something."

"Let me guess. You're all going on an exploration trip to Antarctica to observe the mating rituals of the emperor penguin."

I let out a laugh. "Jas, that's so random. Why would you say that?"

He lifts a shoulder. "Because that would be awesome."

"If you think us girls get together to plan trips to places with sub-zero temperatures, even if it is to see cute little penguins, you really don't know women, Christie."

He waggles his eyebrows at me. "Oh, I know women."

I put my hand up. "I don't want to know."

"So, what did you girls decide?"

"We made a pact. We're calling it the No More Bad Dates Pact, and we're all in on it."

He bites back a smile. Poorly. "The No More Bad Dates Pact? What are you, thirteen?"

"I didn't date at thirteen."

"I did."

"No, you didn't."

"Okay, you got me. I *wanted* to date at thirteen. Vanessa O'Reagan." His eyes get misty. "She was at my high school. Four years older than me and just about the most perfect specimen of womanhood my young eyes had seen."

"Four years is a huge age gap, especially when you're thirteen."

"Didn't you date a guy five years older than you last year?"

"That's totally different, and you know it. We're in our twenties. Thirteen and seventeen is a whole other ball game. A whole other kind of totally creepy ball game."

"Things could never be creepy with Vanessa O'Reagan. Only utterly and completely beautiful." He gets that far-off look in his eyes again before his face creases into a grin.

"When you finally shake yourself out of your walk down pubescent crush lane, shall we get back to the pact?"

"Ah, yes. Back to this incredibly mature pact you three made tonight. Does it involve Chinese burns, noogies, and wedgies? 'Cos that could really add a certain *je ne sais quoi*."

"And you think *I'm* the immature one?" Hope swells inside me as I think about our pact. "It's going to be so good, Jas. We've agreed we're only going to date the good ones. No jerks, idiots, or a-holes need apply."

"How are you going to manage that?"

"We're going to help each other. If one of us meets a guy we want to date, the other two have to meet him to ensure he's worthy."

"Worthy, huh?"

"Yes. *Worthy*. We're worth it, and we've got each other's backs here."

He studies my face for a moment. "Girl code, huh? You've got it all figured out, haven't you?"

"Yes, we have."

"And you don't need any help?"

"I've got my girls, Christie. What more do I need?"

"How about a guy's perspective?"

"What do you mean?"

"Well, you may have noticed I'm a guy."

"I get daily proof of that fact with the towels on the floor and the dishes on the counter."

"And here I was thinking you were going to mention my manly presence, all brooding, strong, and silent."

I let out a laugh. "You are many things, but brooding, strong, and silent you are not."

"Hey! I take that as an insult to my manhood."

I count my points off on my fingers. "First up, you're one of the most annoyingly chirpy people I've ever met, even first thing in the morning. So, you're not in the least bit brooding."

"Accepted."

"Secondly, you can talk more than me! And that's saying something because I'm a girl, and it's kinda in the job description to talk."

"Okay, you got me with that one, too. What about the strong part? I am super strong. Watch." He collects the coffee machine in his hands and lifts it up, only for it to come to an abrupt halt when the cord goes taut, making a twanging sound. "Darn wall plug," he mutters.

I shake my head at him. With an athletic build and at just over six feet tall, there's no denying Jason is in great shape. Despite the fact he's a trainee doctor and works completely crazy long hours, he always finds the time to work out, plus he totally scored in the genes department. "Okay. You're strong. But brooding and silent are off the table."

He shrugs. "I'm happy with that. *Anyway*, my point about this pact thing of yours is that I could give you a guy's perspective."

"How?"

"I could help vet these guys. Make sure they're good enough for you."

I try not to let warmth inside my belly spread at his words. Yup, you guessed it, I fail. You see, Jason is one of my BFFs, and he's always looking out for me. What's more, he's cute. Like *really* cute. Cute in that total smokehouse way. Plenty of women would kill for the chance to be with him (well, maybe not kill exactly. This isn't *Game of Thrones*, but you get the picture). Despite his evident hotness, I can just be myself around him. Hang out, chew the fat. With me and Jason, there's no pretense, no dating nerves.

I scrunch up my nose. "You don't have to do that for me."

"I know. I want to. It'll be fun. Did you decide how it'll work, whether there are any ground rules, that kind of thing?"

"What we've agreed is that we're not going to go on any dates until we've done some checks on the guy."

He raises his eyebrows. "Checks?"

"Nothing hardcore. No police records or anything. Just ask around, check social media, that kind of thing."

"Sounds reasonable. What else?"

"We can only date guys who are willing to meet with the Vetting Committee first. Kind of like a 'what are your intentions toward my daughter' questionnaire."

Jason shakes his head. "You may as well all just give up now and become old maids."

"What? Why?"

"Because no guy is ever going to agree to meeting a girl's friends before he even goes on a date with her."

"He would if he was a nice guy," I reply defensively.

"Or if he thought he might prefer one of the friends."

"Jason M. Christie, I cannot believe you just said that."

He shrugs. "I know the way guys think. That's why you need me. And it's *Doctor* Jason M. Christie to you."

Despite the smile that teases at the edges of his mouth, I know he has a point—not about the doctor part because he's only in training—but about understanding how guys think. Or *don't* think, as the case may be. Pointing out the obvious, Erin, Darcy, and I are all women, trying to navigate the dating warfare landscape. Having a guy friend help us understand the "enemy" might give us an advantage.

"Look," I lay my hands palm down on the counter, "if I say yes to this, you'll need to be a proper part of the team. You're not in charge, you're just one voice."

"Who do you think I am, Genghis Khan?"

"Genghis Khan?" I laugh. "What you do in your spare time is no concern of mine, Christie. If that means dressing up as an all-conquering Chinese emperor, then as long as no one gets hurt . . ."

"Your comedic talent is wasted as a barista, you know, McCarthy."

"I know. I could do so many incredible things with my life. Now, promise you're not going to come in and try to take over."

"I'm not going to come in and try to take over."

Satisfied, I nod. "You're on the team."

He studies my face for a beat, then says, "You're serious about this, huh? You want to meet the right guy."

"I do. I've had enough of the wrong ones, the ones I don't particularly care about, the ones who definitely don't care about me. I want—" I stop myself from going on.

"What?"

"No, you'll think I'm silly."

"How do you know I don't already think that?"

"Do you?"

"No. Far from it. Tell me."

"I want to be with someone I'm so into I can barely breathe, you know?"

"That sounds more like a respiratory condition to me, McCarthy. And I would know, I'm—"

"—a doctor," I finish for him. "As you remind me ten times a day, every day. Although, for some reason, you forget to add the word 'trainee' when you mention it."

"Semantics, McCarthy. Semantics. So, back to this respiratory condition," he leads with a smirk on his face I know too well.

I roll my eyes. "You have no romance in your soul, Christie. It's that Ariana Grande song. The line is about falling for someone so hard you can hardly even breathe."

"I don't listen to Ariana Grande. I'm a twenty-seven-year-old man."

"Everyone listens to Ariana Grande, whether you know you are or not. She's everywhere." I stifle a yawn. "All right. I'm going to bed. I need my beauty sleep. With Bailey only just back from her honeymoon, I've been getting one day off a week and I've got a Mandatory McCarthy Meal tomorrow." I collect my glass from the counter to take to my room.

"You've always got Mandatory McCarthy Meals."

I'm from a large Irish Catholic family—is there any other kind of Irish Catholic family?—and most weeks, Mom puts a call out to her offspring, their partners, kids, and various hangers-on to attend a Sunday family lunch: the "Mandatory McCarthy Meal." They're usually raucous affairs with my family's seemingly huge ability to talk loudly and offer opinions on everything, so unless you want to have every aspect of your life dissected and "fixed," it's best to keep your personal business to yourself. The last thing I'm going to do tomorrow is mention my new pact.

Jason jumps off the counter. "Good night, Soph. We'll start plotting tomorrow."

"Am I going to regret this?" I ask.

"Never," Jason replies with a wink.

As I make my way down the hallway to my bedroom, I seriously begin to wonder if I will.

Chapter 3

As I finish applying my mascara the following morning, there's a knock on my bedroom door. "You decent?" Jason calls out.

I screw the lid onto my mascara and pick up my lipstick. "My lips aren't dressed yet, but other than that, absolutely."

He pushes the door open and leans up against the door jamb. "I can handle naked lips. Even though it sounds weird to call them 'naked.' That means my lips are naked, like, all the time, right?"

I apply my lipstick and then look at his reflection in the mirror. "Lipstick would look totally weird on you, Jas."

"I'll take that as a compliment. So, what time are we due at lunch?"

I turn to look at him with raised eyebrows. "*We're* not due anywhere. *I'm* going to *my* family lunch just as soon as I put on my jacket."

"Well, I've got a text from Mammy McCarthy here that tells me otherwise." He waves his phone in the air. "*We'd love to see you, Jason,*" he begins in a terrible rendition of my mom's Irish lilt as he reads his screen. "*You know how much we adore you.*" He looks up at me with a grin on his face. "See? Your mom adores me. Mammy McCarthy clearly has great taste and clearly wants me to come to the Mandatory McCarthy Meal."

I shake my head and smile. "Only because you flirt your butt off with her every time you see her." I slip my jean jacket on and sling my purse over my shoulder.

"Can I help it if the older ladies have a thing for me? No, Sophie, I cannot. And anyway, I haven't had a Sunday off in over a month. Some of your mom's cooking would suit me just nicely."

"Well," I say with a chuckle, "I guess you're coming with me, then."

A short drive later, we pull up outside my old family home in a suburb not far from our downtown apartment. As we get out of my beat-up old car, I glance at the expensive Europeans parked against the curb. "My brother and sisters are here already."

He whistles. "Is that Sean's new car?"

"You mean the shiny one that looks all dark and threatening? Yup, that's totally my brother's style."

"Maybe your car will grow up to be like his one day?"

"I can only hope." My voice positively oozes sarcasm. Being like my brother, Sean, is not exactly on my list of to-dos.

"Since you're the youngest, aren't you given more leeway? Daddy's little girl and all that?"

I push open the fence and walk up the path to my parents' front door. "I'm not a daddy's girl."

"Oh, you so are. And I don't blame you. I'd be a daddy's girl if I had Pappy McCarthy as my dad."

Jason has always referred to my parents as "Mammy" and "Pappy" McCarthy. I think he got it from some Netflix show he watched about an Irish crime gang or something. More than once I've had to explain to him that we McCarthys are just a regular family with absolutely no links to the Irish mafia underworld—no matter how much he wants us to be.

As I push my way through the yellow front door, I'm hit by the chatter of voices emanating from down the hall, the aroma of my mom's famous bacon and cabbage with the best roast potatoes you'll ever eat filling my nostrils. I know bacon and cabbage sounds truly,

truly horrible, but cooked right, the Irish way that Mom does it, it's delicious. Although you may have to simply trust me on that.

I stand in the doorway and take in the scene before me. As always, Mom is stirring something on the stove, giving her firm opinion on something to my sister Abigail. Dad is leaning back in his chair at the kitchen table, one of the last people on the planet to read an actual newspaper, his reading glasses balanced on the end of his nose. He's flanked by Sean, my one and only brother, who has his back to me as he talks on his phone and stares out the glass door onto the back yard.

My other siblings are two sisters, Caitlin and Fiona, and they're nowhere to be seen, but I can hear them in the living room with Caitlin's baby daughter, Lola, and Sean's son, Simon.

And then there are the partners: two husbands, a long-term boyfriend, and a wife for Sean. My family. A whole cartload of 'em.

"Hey, everyone," I say.

Mom looks up from her cooking. "*Mo stoirín*," she says, using one of her favorite Irish terms of endearment as her eyes crinkle with her warm smile.

"That always sounds to me like she's saying, 'must Doreen,' and I wonder who the heck Doreen is," Jason says quietly into my ear.

I give him a quick eye roll before greeting my family, one by one, each and every last one of them. It takes some time, I can tell you, because there's a lot of us.

"Jason, how wonderful to see you, love," Mom coos and blushes as Jason gives her a kiss on the cheek.

"The pleasure is all mine, Siobhan, I promise you. You look extra gorgeous today. Is that a new blouse?" he asks.

"Oh, Jason," Mom replies as her face flushes.

I shake my head at his blatant flirtation. Jason could charm the pants off a roomful of committed, elderly nuns.

"When you two have finished your mutual admiration session, will you bring that wooden board with the soda bread out to the table," Dad says to Jason.

"Of course," Jason replies smoothly. "You're looking very dapper today, Pappy McCarthy. Have you lost weight?"

And so Jason continues, charming my entire family—the youngest members included with tickles and funny faces, much to their delight—until Mom mercifully announces that lunch is ready. We take our seats at the dining room table on a mish-mash of chairs. The table my parents bought way back in the Dark Ages— okay, the eighties—was never designed to accommodate all of us McCarthys and hangers-on at once. Today, I get the creaky swivel chair from Dad's office down the hall, and I've got to pump it up so I'm not the size of a ten-year-old child next to my siblings and their partners.

As we sit together at the table, we serve ourselves up cabbage with chunky bacon and enough roast potatoes and gravy to feed the entire New Zealand-Irish population. There's general chit-chat about babies and house renovations and what's growing well in the veggie patch right now. Apparently, the snails are on attack and the spinach has been ruined, much to everyone's dismay.

Talk turns to Sean and Fiona's legal practice, McCarthy & McCarthy, and how they have too many clients so they'll need to employ another lawyer soon just to keep up; to Abigail's latest success as marketing manager at the tech company she works for; and finally, how amazingly well Caitlin's new online baby store, Baby-ness, is doing in the breast pump sector. These successes are all well and good, but I ask you, is breast pumping an appropriate conversation while consuming food?

With all my siblings' recent achievements fogging up the room, inevitably, the conversation turns to me and the state of my life.

Which is just awesome.

"What's happening with you, Sophie?" Mom says from the other end of the table, and all eyes in the room turn to me. Even the babies swivel their heads to stare at me. No word of a lie.

"Well, I'm enjoying work." My mind turns to the Cozy Cottage Café. I love it there. It's got such a great feel to the place, so relaxed and welcoming. It's like being at home, snuggled up in your favorite armchair but with the yummiest food and an endless supply of coffee. Sure, it's where I work, but seriously, there's something about the café that makes your worries melt away when you walk through the door.

"Are you still at that café?" Sean can't keep the judgment from his voice. "I thought you were going to work for some tech company or something?"

"No, it was a telco. I'm sure of it." Abigail says.

"You're both wrong. It was a power company. Nettco," Caitlin says with authority. "I was the one who set it up."

"Nettco? Aren't they government-owned?" Sean asks.

"Whatever sort of business this company is in," Dad interrupts in his authoritative way, "it clearly wasn't the right place for our Sophie." He winks at me. "Was it, love?" Dad is the sweet Kiwi-Irish guy who fell in love and married the Irish *cailín* while on a jaunt to Dublin way back when.

Jason nudges me with his elbow. "How are you not a daddy's girl?" he whispers and receives a glare from me.

"No." I let out a puff of air and force a smile. I'd gone to an interview at Nettco last week, more to please my "all up in my business" siblings than any real desire to start a career in the electricity industry. They didn't offer me the job, and I didn't lose a whole lot of sleep over it.

"What went wrong?" Fiona asks.

I open my mouth to respond but am interrupted by Abigail. "Do you need some interview skills training? I could put you through your paces, teach you a thing or two."

"Abigail's right, Sophie. It's very important to know how to interview," Fiona says with a sage nod. "Do you know how to interview well?"

I open my mouth to speak when Sean waves my sister's idea away. "Oh, she doesn't need that. She needs experience. Actual working experience. If she can't get a paid job, she needs to become an intern somewhere. Methink'st working as a barista doesn't exactly teach you how to think, does it, Sophie?"

"Methink'st" is one of Sean's favorite words, and he totally overuses it. But then let's face it, using the word "methink'st" even just once is overusing it, really.

Taken from old Willie Shakespeare himself, I've often thought Sean only uses such words and expressions because he thinks they make him sound all learned and clever. I wonder whether people even understand him. I mean, what exactly are "froward and unable worms," anyway? Worms that lie around in the garden on little deckchairs, watching Netflix all day?

Jason, who up until this point has been a silent observer in the conversation, pipes up with, "Sophie happens to make the best latte this side of the Bombay Hills, you know. That is a real skill."

I shoot him a small smile of gratitude, and he flashes me his dazzling Jason version back.

Sean scoffs. "We're talking *careers* here, Jason. Making a good coffee is all well and good, but where will Sophie be in five years? Ten? Behind the counter, serving up cappuccinos?"

"That's a good point, you know, Sean," Fiona says. "I've got an idea: Sophie, you could move back home and take a job as an intern at McCarthy & McCarthy. Couldn't she, Sean? We need help right now with all these new clients, and Sophie has a finance degree, so we all know she can pick things up quickly."

"What an excellent notion," Sean says.

I blink at them in disbelief. Move back home? Work with my brother and sister at their stuffy old legal practice? Are they freaking *kidding* me with this?

It becomes the straw that broke the camel's back, and as the camel in this equation, I've had enough of this conversation.

"Thanks, everyone, for your ideas," I say in what I hope is a sweet but firm "don't mess with me" tone. Really this whole "fix Sophie" thing is getting out of control. They bring it up every Mandatory McCarthy Meal, and I'm officially over it. "I want you all to know I'm very happy where I am right now. I love the work I do at the Cozy Cottage, my bosses are awesome, and I've got no plans to work as an intern or move home."

"That's good to hear. I don't want to have to find a new room-mate," Jason says with a wink.

I roll my eyes at him as Dad echoes my words with his own. "Sophie's right. She's doing just fine, aren't you, love?" He smiles at me, and I nod. "You're all very sweet the way you want to look after your baby sister, but remember, some of you took a while to get your careers off the ground, too. You weren't doing what you wanted when you just graduated in your early twenties. So, give her time. She'll get there, won't you, love?"

"Oh, you are so a daddy's girl," Jason whispers in my ear.

"Err, Dad? Sophie's twenty-five," Caitlin adds helpfully, which wins a swift kick under the table from me. "Ow! What was that for?" she complains.

Dad's speech is so sweet and supportive, none of us should need to bother him with semantics like my age or the fact I graduated from college three years ago. Minor, irrelevant details.

His shaggy gray eyebrows shoot up. "You're twenty-five?" he asks me, and I give a reluctant nod. He looks at Mom at the other end of the table. "Where does the time go, love?"

"I don't know myself. What I do know is with all this talk about our Sophie, no one's eating nearly enough of this meal I spent hours preparing for you all."

"Sorry, Mom," Sean, always the biggest suck-up with our mom, says, and obediently, we all set about devouring our meals.

Thankfully, the conversation moves onto other topics for the rest of lunch, and I'm let off the hook—at least for today.

You see, this is the problem with not only being the baby of the family—a "pleasant surprise" as my parents refer to me, otherwise known as a whoopsy in the contraception department five years after their last child was born—but I'm also the only one with no real direction in life. I know it, they know it, and I'd really rather prefer to bury my head in the sand about the whole thing.

⊂══⊃

LATER, in the car on the way home, I know Jason's going to bring the "let's fix Sophie" conversation up again.

"Okay, Soph, tell me: when you move back home, how do you want your old bedroom decorated? Pastel pink with unicorns and rainbows? Oh, wait, that's how it looks *now*."

"No, it doesn't!" I protest. "Well, there aren't any unicorns, anyway."

"Ha! You're such a girl."

"You make it sound like it's a bad thing."

"It's not. It's merely an observation, that's all. Anyway, back to your family's constant need to 'fix' you," he leads. "What's all that about?"

I grip onto the steering wheel as I pull up at a red light. "I don't know. They've all got their lives sorted out, I guess. Sean and Fiona both knew they wanted to be lawyers, practically from when they were in diapers. Caitlin always wanted to run her own business, and now she's like the Kim Kardashian of baby clothes."

"Don't forget the breast pumps."

I giggle. "Yeah, and Queen of Breast Pump-onia."

"You know, from a guy's perspective the whole pumping milk out of your breasts thing is super weird. I mean, breasts are easily among my favorite things. I'm not sure I want to think about cows' udders when I'm, you know, visiting a pair."

"*Visiting a pair?*" I let out a laugh. "That's quite a turn of phrase you got there, Christie."

"What would you prefer I said?"

"Actually, I don't want to think about you and breasts, be they cow's udders or otherwise. Roommate, remember? But I promise, when you have that nurse from last night back, I'll be sure not to make any mooing noises to put you off your game."

"That would be much appreciated. And no cow bells, either," he deadpans.

"Definitely no cow bells."

We fall silent for a couple of blocks until Jason, dog with a bone that he is, returns to the lunchtime conversation once more. "The way I see it, it's your life. If you want to be a barista, then go for it. You're the one who needs to be happy."

I indicate to turn and wait for an oncoming car to zip by. "Here's the thing: I'm not sure it *is* what I want to do. Don't get me wrong, I love the Cozy Cottage, I love the girls there, and I know I make a good coffee."

"You make the best coffee, Soph. I only wish the hospital were closer. I'd be there all the time."

"You'd get fat on Bailey's amazing cakes."

"Bring it."

I let out a sigh. "I don't know. I took the job after I graduated and I guess it was good enough that I just got stuck, you know?" I spy a parking spot near our apartment block and reverse into it.

"Well, three years on, maybe it's time to get *un*stuck?"

The thought of leaving the safe, comfortable harbor of the Cozy Cottage sits uncomfortably inside. "And do what?"

Jason pushes the passenger door open with his foot. "Whatever you want." He gets out of the car and closes the door.

I sit, lost in thought. As much as I've loved my time at the café, maybe Jason and my family are right? Maybe it's time to "unstuck" myself? Maybe it's time to brave something new?

The thought scares me half to death.

Chapter 4

I push open the heavy back door to the Cozy Cottage Café and step inside. Despite the fact it's still early, the kitchen is a hive of activity, the most delectable smells wafting through the air, making my empty belly grumble. My bosses, Bailey and Paige, are the best bakers in the city, possibly even the whole country, and I'm not bragging. The Cozy Cottage is known for its cakes, and everyone seems to have a favorite. Me? I like them all, and right now I could eat an entire cake all to myself. Seriously, there should be a public service announcement about this place: if you work here, your waistline will be in perilous danger.

"Morning," I say as I hang my jacket up and don one of the Cozy Cottage Café's trademark frilled, pink aprons with white polka dots.

Paige looks up at me from the cake she's decorating—carrot cake, by the looks of the thick, creamy frosting—and grins. "Sophie! Great to see you. Good weekend?"

Before I can stop it, my mind instantly darts to the "Sophie's life intervention" I got to experience, courtesy of my brother and sisters yesterday. Despite my best efforts to avoid even thinking about an unpaid internship at one of my siblings' companies—not to mention moving back home, the idea of which makes me shudder like jelly in a violent earthquake—I know I'm going nowhere with my life.

I give her a breezy smile. "I went to karaoke with the girls on Saturday night."

"Fun! What did you sing?"

"'Stronger.' You know, the Kelly Clarkson song?"

"Oh." She stands up and looks at me, assessing me with her big eyes. "An angry song, huh?"

"It's not an angry song. It's a song about overcoming adversity and coming out the other end better. Stronger."

"Okay. Sure." She nods at me with a weird-looking smile on her face, like she just swallowed an oyster. I hate oysters.

"I'm not angry anymore, if that's what you're thinking. I am over it. Over. It. Trust me."

"I wasn't thinking anything," Paige replies with a shrug. "Just as long as you had fun. That's a great song, for whatever reason you chose it."

It's a cryptic response, one that has me trying to work out whether she agreed with me or not. I'm still puzzled when Bailey comes bustling into the kitchen with an empty tray. "That cake ready for slicing?" she asks Paige. "Oh, hi there, Sophie. Good weekend?"

"Sophie sang 'Stronger' at karaoke," Paige announces, her face impassive.

"'Stronger?'" Bailey's eyebrows rise to meet her hairline.

"Kelly Clarkson," Paige adds.

My two bosses share a look before Bailey turns to me and says "Oh, Sophie" in a tone that inexplicably makes me want to cry. Which is crazy because I'm so over what Andrew did to me. I know it was a jerk move to dump me in the church, and I know I'm worth ten of him (Dad says fifty, although I'm choosing to be a little less gung-ho about it all). But . . . there's always a "but," and that's what bothers me.

And my sweet, empathetic, almost freaking psychic bosses know it.

"Look. I'm fine," I say with a shrug to show them both just how incredibly fine I am about it all. Incredibly, totally, and utterly fine. "I am. Honestly. I'm good now. It's all in the past. Move on dot com, that's where I'm at. #OverIt."

There's an outside chance I'm laying it on a little too thick here.

Bailey scrunches up her nose. "Are you sure? Because it's totally fine if you're not."

"One hundred percent. In fact, I took a leaf out of your book on Saturday night. Out of both your books."

"You baked?" Bailey asks with a twinkle in her eye.

"I've told you before: my role in life outside of being your favorite barista is to *eat* the cakes, not bake them," I say with a smile. "My friends and I agreed to a pact. A little like the one you were all in on a couple years back."

Paige's jaw drops open, and her hand flies to her chest. "The One Last First Date Pact? You want to find The One?"

"Kind of. I mean, sure, I'd like to find The One someday. But for now, we all agreed we'd like to just date good guys, avoid the jerks. No more Andrew Fosters, I guess."

"That's almost as good as One Last First Date Pact, don't you think, Bailey?"

She laughs. "Sophie, you so deserve to date the good ones. You've had some bad luck in the men department."

I square my shoulders, bolstered by her words. "I do. You're right. Us women often accept less than good enough. I'm guilty of it, and so are my friends. I mean, Darcy dated a guy last year who she didn't even like! So now, we're making a stand: no more bad dates."

"Is that what you're calling your pact?" Bailey asks.

I nod, adding, "No jerks need apply."

Paige claps her hands together. "The No More Bad Dates Pact. So cute!"

"I know, right? Starting from now, we're not accepting anything less than the good guys." I stand tall. This feels good. No, scratch that: this feels great. So what if my family thinks I'm stuck in a dead-end job, in need of a life makeover? At least I'm in control of one thing in my life. And I have a feeling this pact is going to work for Darcy, Erin, and me, just the way the One Last First Date Pact did for them.

"Good for you. How are you doing it?" Paige asks. "Are you vetting them first? Most of us did that, it was a really great idea. No wolves in sheep's clothing."

"We're definitely vetting them, are you kidding me? It's Darcy, Erin, and me," I reply. "Oh, and Jason, my roommate, too."

"The really cute one you tried to set Bailey up with ages ago?" Paige asks.

It's true. Back before Bailey and Ryan fell in love, I thought she and Jason might make a good match. The fact I had a crush on Ryan at the time had nothing to do with it. Honestly.

"What you mean is he's the one who looks a little like your husband, right?" I reply with a laugh.

Paige is *so* transparent. She fell hard for Josh a couple or more years back, and their wedding was whimsical and romantic, just like Bailey's.

And, most importantly, no one dumped me during her wedding service, which is now the low bar I've begun to judge weddings by. Sad, right? So, so sad.

"Yeah, okay. The one who looks like Josh," Paige concedes. "I think it's great that you're getting a guy's perspective on this whole pact thing. We never had that."

"That's what Jason said."

"It'll be fun to vet his potential dates."

I shake my head. "Oh, no. He's not in on the pact in that way. He's just helping out, that's all."

Paige raises her eyebrows as she studies my face. "Interesting."

I shift, uncomfortable. "How's that interesting? He's my roomie so he's got a vested interest in me not dating any more jerks."

She shrugs. "I guess. Do you have anyone in mind for the first date?"

"Not yet." Hope bubbles up inside me, and I can't help but smile. "But I'm hoping it won't take long."

Paige looks at her watch. "Do you think you can delay looking for this good guy of yours? I need the coffee machine prepped before the early morning coffee and muffin brigade beats down our door in only about ten minutes' time."

"Of course!" I say, giddy with my new-found confidence. "I'm on it."

The café is busier than usual, even for a Monday, and we're kept working hard making coffee, toasting bagels, and serving up muffins right through to the coffee and cake crew, who begin to turn up right around ten.

To my surprise, Jason is one of them, accompanied by a group of people I've not met before. One of them is a very pretty blonde girl with a high ponytail and the kind of ski jump nose I always wanted as a kid.

Yeah, okay, I still do.

He reaches across the counter and taps me on the shoulder, almost making me drop the jug of hot milk I'm busy frothing.

"Are you the famous Cozy Cottage barista I've heard all about through the Irish mafia network?"

I laugh. "Jas. What are you doing here?"

"I had a hankering for a coffee and some cake. You sell that here, right?"

I shake my head at him. "You're a comedian, you know that?" I return my attention to the milk, which is point blank refusing to froth. Milk is temperamental. It's one of the life lessons I've gained as a barista. If you don't treat it right, it will let you down. And with the number of lattes and cappuccinos and flat whites I've got on my list right now, the last thing I need is moody milk.

"Hi, Bailey," I hear Jason say.

"Oh. Hi, there. Jason, right?" she replies.

I pull back far enough so I can observe their interaction. For some reason, Jason never fails to rattle Bailey, and she usually reacts by running the other way.

"What can I get you?" she asks him.

"I've heard you've got the best barista in town at this café, so I'm gonna need a whole load of coffees." He lists the group's coffee order out for Bailey, adding a slice of the various cakes on offer for all his friends.

Then he and his friends take some seats by the window, Ski Jump Nose gazing at Jason like he's a piece of one of Bailey's cakes himself.

I roll my eyes. Typical. Maybe it's the doctor thing, or maybe it's because he looks like he could be a Hollywood actor, but Jason always gets the pretty girls. The confident girls I look at and know I'll never be like. They're too put together, too focused, too everything. And, as was established with extreme precision at the Mandatory McCarthy Meal, I am the opposite of all that: a mess, completely *un*focused, and not a whole lot more.

"Here you are," Bailey says as she tacks a fresh list of coffees to the machine. "That'll keep you busy for a while."

I scan the list. "Sure will."

Paige walks out of the kitchen and slips a fresh cake into the cabinet next to me. "Hey, I might have a guy in mind for you," she says, her face beaming.

"You do?" I say in surprise.

"That was fast, even for you, Paige." This from Bailey.

"What's the point in waiting?" she says with a shrug. "His name is Oliver Price. He's a good guy. We used to work together at A.G.D., back before I saw the light and left the corporate world for the café."

I press the button to grind some fresh coffee beans. "Look, I appreciate the offer, really I do. But I'm not sure I should have my boss setting me up on a date. Boundaries, and all that."

"Boundaries schmoundaries," Paige says with a flick of her wrist. "You said you were serious about this pact, and I've helped my friends find their perfect matches, as well as had some serious luck in the love department myself. I guess you could say I've got pedigree."

"Pedigree?" Bailey questions with a chuckle.

"Yes, pedigree," Paige insists. "Although the way you said it you make me sound like a prize dog."

"You are not a prize dog, Paige," Bailey says. "Just a hopeless romantic."

"I am a hopeless romantic, it's true. I can't help myself."

Paige and her husband Josh are so loved-up, they've got to be the cutest couple I've ever seen. It's enough to make me want to find love myself—or vomit. The jury's still out on that one right now.

I load up the coffee arm and slot it into place. "I'm not sure, Paige. Setups never work out."

"Sure they do," Paige replies.

"Like for whom?" Bailey asks. "Name me one couple who got set up and fell in love."

"Me and Josh." Paige shoots us a triumphant grin.

"That was different. You knew him already when Marissa and I set you up with him. I mean a blind date setup."

Paige twists her lips as she thinks. "Okay, you got me. Maybe Sophie and Oliver could be the first couple who met on a blind date and makes it?"

"Well, if I were single and looking for non-jerk guys to date, I'd ask that guy out." Bailey gestures at a man sitting on his own at one of the tables.

"Oh, yeah. He's cute in a Clark Kent kind of way," Paige agrees. "Right down to those glasses of his."

"Stop it! You'll have us picturing him ripping them off as he transforms into Superman." Bailey waggles her eyebrows at me, and I roll my eyes.

"Bailey, you're already married to a superhero." I pour some fresh milk into a jug.

Bailey shakes her head. "Ryan might be the best husband I could ever imagine, but he's no superhero."

"That's right. He only *looks* like Thor." Paige smiles as she nudges me.

"Anyway, focusing here, ladies," Bailey says. I assume she's telling us to get to work, so I'm surprised when she goes on to say, "That Clark Kent lookalike comes in here all the time. He's always alone and always orders the same thing. I think he's lonely and looking for love."

I laugh. "Isn't that a bit of a leap?"

Bailey shrugs. "Maybe. But wouldn't it be fun finding out?"

"Sophie's not looking for love, remember? Are you, Sophie?" Paige has a gleam in her eye.

They both look at me with interest. I shrug. "If it happens, sure. But mostly I just want to date non-jerks."

"See?" Paige's eyes are dancing. "Forget Clark Kent. Go on a date with Oliver. He's really cute, he's single, which I know because I just checked his social media in between frosting cakes, and he's all about photos of him with the guys right now. Not a girl in sight. And, most importantly, he's a non-jerk, I promise."

A peal of laughter floats across the café. I look over at Jason and see Ski Jump Nose's hand on his arm as she laughs at whatever he's saying.

I'm not sure what it is—the fact my roommate has yet another girlfriend or maybe the way in which she's obviously so delighted to be with him—but somehow it kicks me into life. With my nonexistent career, the pressure my siblings put me under to pull my life together, and the fact that even I would have to admit I'm treading water, I *need* this.

"You know what? I made this pact with my girlfriends because I want to date the right kinds of guys. So, why not? I'd love to meet this Oliver guy."

Paige hops up and down on the spot and makes a noise that sounds like a velociraptor's squeal. "Oh, Sophie. You are not going to regret this."

I so hope she's right.

Chapter 5

My phone vibrates in my back pocket, and I pull it out to check who's messaging me. It's from Sean with his usual short, sharp and to the point communication style.

Family dinner at my place tonight. 7 o'clock. Don't be late.

I hold my phone in my hands, my thumbs hovering over the keypad. I'd like to tell him to go stick it, maybe send him a message telling him not to be so darn bossy. But I know I won't. He's my big brother, and I know his heart is in the right place. And anyway, family is very important to me, no matter how much they sometimes drive me insane.

I tap out a quick reply, asking if I should bring something, but knowing his wife, Danni, she will have it all worked out. All I've got to do is turn up and eat. Oh, and get my life totally rearranged in the process. In "The World According to Sean," I'm a successful whatever, earning "good money" to pay off my mortgage and run my European car, a fully contributing member of society.

So boring, so him, and so not me.

Once at Sean's house in the leafy suburb of Remuera, Abigail thrusts a glass of red wine into my hand. "Sophie, we've got a plan."

The bushes are clearly free from being beaten tonight. There's nothing like getting straight to the point.

I look around at my four siblings, their faces grave and full of concern for me. It would be touching, lovely even, if I didn't already know what was coming next. I take a large gulp of my wine and then another. Dutch courage? Heck yes.

Sean holds court. "We've got options for you. Not like the last time with that Nettco interview Abigail set up for you. This time, you get to choose which step up you want to take."

"Because that's what this is, Soph—a step up." Caitlin gives me that familiar look that says, "you need all the help we can give you, don't you, our poor little Sophie."

I'm a little too familiar with that look.

"Okaaay." I look around at my sibling's faces. "Well? What are these options you're talking about? I'm super eager to know." There's a chance I'm not being one hundred percent honest here.

"You are?" Caitlin sounds surprised.

"Of course! The last job you put me forward for wasn't a good fit, that's all. And the one before that wasn't a good fit either, I guess. And the one before that was—"

"Not a good fit?" Abigail offers, the ghost of a smile on her face.

"Well, clearly! I didn't want to work at a fast-food chain." I cross my arms, defensive. I know my brother and sisters are looking out for me, and I know they've come up with some solid suggestions for career choices in the past. But none of them have floated my boat, and I figured why leave a place I love, even if I'm "only a barista" as Sean likes to say, to go somewhere I know I'll hate?

"That job was on the managerial track," Fiona says, clearly indignant. The fast-food chain position had been her idea. "Jimmy said you'd be managing a team within six months tops."

"Fiona, it was flipping burgers." I shoot her a look. "I've got nothing against flipping burgers, it's just I didn't want to do it."

"Only to start with. That job had potential." Abigail leans back in her seat and crosses her arms.

I've affronted her. "Look, I'm sorry. You're right, Fiona. It was really nice of you to get me the intro there. I'm sorry it didn't work out."

Sean leans forward and rests his elbows on his knees. "Sophie. You're bright and you're educated. That's two big ticks in your favor. All we want is for you to find something you want to do, something that can become an actual career. We all have them," he gestures to our sisters, "and we could not be happier. Right?"

"Right," Caitlin echoes as Abigail says, "Absolutely," and Fiona gives a firm nod.

"Having a meaningful career will give you so much in your life," Sean carries on. And on. And on. Did I mention my brother loves the sound of his own voice? When he eventually "shakes off this mortal coil," to coin another one of his beloved Shakespearean expressions, his epitaph will be "Everyone is entitled to my opinion." And you know what? I bet he'd agree, without even a hint of irony.

"Okay, thanks, everyone," I say to stop Sean from waffling on endlessly. Really, how does Danni put up with him? I mean I've got to because we're related. She *chose* him. "I get it. You want me to have a 'meaningful existence.'" I use air quotes. "I do, too. It's just . . . I guess I don't know what that looks like yet."

"It's because you're totally stuck," Abigail says with a sage nod.

"Exactly, you're stuck like a pig in mud," Caitlin confirms.

"Isn't a pig in mud someone who's really happy?" I say, immediately regretting it.

"Deflecting isn't going to help you here, Sophie," Caitlin warns. "This is an intervention."

"Yup, I got that." I grin as I rub my hands together. "So, intervene away!"

"Take this seriously, please," Abigail says.

"I am. Sorry. I'm keen to hear how you're going to transform my humdrum existence."

"Well, as you know, Baby-ness has gone from strength to strength," Caitlin begins with a smile on her face as she names her online baby store. "Profits are up, and we're shipping more and more product. Which brings me to one of the options we want to put forward to you, Sophie." She pauses for dramatic effect before announcing, "I would like you to come and work for me at Baby-ness."

My eyes widen. "Really?"

The thought of working for Caitlin isn't exactly appealing.

"Yes. Wouldn't that be amazing? I'll teach you everything I know."

"Err, yes. That would be—" What? Horrendous? Slit-my-wrists terrible? All of the above? "—*so* amazing. Thank you."

"Or," Sean flashes a smile at Fiona, "you could come work at McCarthy & McCarthy as our intern. I know your degree is in finance, not law, but we could definitely use your skills in dealing with clients and managing the office for us."

Working for Sean and Fiona? *Sean* and Fiona? Think of the amount of Shakespeare I'd have to deal with, let alone being bossed around by them all day, every day.

"Thank you," I manage. But in my head, a big, flashing red sign screams, "Alert! Alert! Pull up! Pull up!"

"Well? What do you think?" Fiona's eyes are full of hope. "I may be biased, but Sean and I think working for us at McCarthy & McCarthy would really suit you. Who knows? You may even decide to go back to school and get that law degree we've often discussed."

The two lawyers in the family, Sean and Fiona, have been pushing me to become a lawyer for years now. They have this fantasy about me joining their firm. What would we call ourselves, McCarthy & McCarthy & McCarthy? It doesn't exactly have a great ring to it, does it?

"Or, you could join Baby-ness. We're new and innovative with an amazingly bright future in the baby and mother wellness arena," Caitlin says.

Sean harrumphs and Caitlin whips her head and glares at him. "We're not all boring old fuddy-duddies, you know. Baby and mother wellness is a growing market, spearheaded by some very big names."

"Until the next fad comes along. Who will spearhead that, I wonder? *Dora the Explorer?*" Sean laughs heartily at his own weak joke.

"There's no need for such a low blow," Abigail says to Sean.

"Thank you," Caitlin sniffs, affronted.

"It could be one Spongebob. He's very wise, I hear." Fiona joins Sean in laughing, and Caitlin crosses her arms and rolls her eyes. She is singularly unimpressed.

"We'll see who gets the last laugh, you two," she quips.

And so the bickering continues, and the point of this so-called "intervention" falls completely by the wayside. I get up from my seat and slink out into the kitchen where I chat to Danni and play peek-a-boo with Simon, my adorable little nephew.

Eventually, once they realize I'm no longer in the room—which takes considerably longer than you'd think—all four of them appear in the kitchen.

"Why did you leave?" Caitlin asks.

"What are you doing in here?" This from Fiona.

"You need to take this seriously, Sophie," Sean chastises.

I look at Abigail for her remark. All she does is raise her hands in the air and shrug at me.

"Look, I appreciate what you're all trying to do. Really, I do."

"Here comes the 'but,'" Fiona says.

I shake my head. "There's no 'but.'"

"So that means you'll come and work at Baby-ness?" The eager expression on Caitlin's face is only matched by Sean's when he says, "Or McCarthy & McCarthy. A much more solid choice, methink'st."

I glance between them both. "Will either of you actually pay me any money?"

"Well, we could down the line. You know, once you've got your feet under the table, settled in, got up to speed." Sean's overuse of ways in which to say "once you know what you're doing" doesn't distract me from the fact that he and Fiona are offering me a job with *no pay*.

I turn my attention to Caitlin.

"Eventually," she says.

Oh, this gets better and better! Working as an *unpaid* intern for any of my siblings is about as appealing as having my hair plucked from my head, strand by painful strand.

I raise a hand in the "stop" sign. "What am I meant to do for money? How will I live?"

"We discussed this, and we think the best thing for you to do would be to move back home," Sean says.

"Exactly. I'm sure Mom and Dad would love to have you back," Fiona adds.

Move back in with my parents? Are they freaking *kidding* me with this right now?

"No way!" It's an utterly preposterous suggestion. I mean, I'm a twenty-five-year-old woman. I've been living away from my parents for the last three years. I'm happy. I like independence. Love my parents as I do, I'm not going to throw all of that away for an internship with one of my siblings.

Abigail, the only non-interested party in the conversation, puts a placating hand on my arm. "Look, Soph, don't go making any hasty decisions right now, okay? Take some time. I suggest you get the two offers on paper so you can see what you'll be doing for each company, then make your decision." She looks up at the others. "You can do that for her, right?" Sean, Fiona, and Caitlin all murmur their assent. "That's settled then. Once you get the details, you can work out what you want. Things will fall into place then. I just know they will."

"Sure," I mumble with a nod.

I'm one hundred and fifty thousand percent positive I don't want to work for Sean and Fiona *or* Caitlin. And three thousand trillion percent positive the very last thing I want to do is move back home to live with Mom and Dad.

Chapter 6

The following day at work, my siblings' offers keep rolling through my mind. I'd rather give up my favorite brand of lip gloss than work for either of their businesses—and if you've ever found that perfect shade with long-lasting ability and low gloop-factor, you'll understand just how serious I am here. But . . . there's a but, and it's chewing on my brain, making it hard to focus on my work.

There's a part of me that admits there's truth to what they said. Not a part of me that feels like *telling* any of them this, but a part all the same. Working at the Cozy Cottage Café has been safe and easy, and I've kind of got myself stuck being a barista, enjoying the work environment, the people. Not feeling like I need to do a whole lot more with my life. All my siblings are super successful and know what they're doing. They've got drive, determination, direction, and all the other d-words that mean they're doing so much better than me.

What am I so darn scared of?

After we've closed the café for the day, I'm sweeping the hallway leading to the bathrooms when the door bursts open and Paige appears. She's holding her hand over her mouth, her eyes bulging as she dashes past me and closes the door to the ladies' with a loud *bang* behind her.

I knit my eyebrows together. Is she sick? She sure looked green around the edges from the blur I saw on her way down the hall.

It's none of my business so I get on with my task of sweeping up. My mind begins to wander as I work. Maybe it's one of the cakes? Or the chicken we use in the toasted paninis? I say a little prayer it's not the chicken; I ate two sandwiches with it today, and the last thing I need to add to my directionless, dateless, treading-water existence is food poisoning.

A few moments later, Paige reappears at the door. She looks a little less green, but definitely not out of the vomit woods yet.

I rest my broom up against the wall and ask, "Are you okay?"

"I think so."

"Did you eat the chicken? Please, don't say it's the chicken."

She shakes her head. "It's not the chicken."

I let out a relieved puff of air. "Thank goodness. One of the cakes? Was the cream cheese off?"

Again, she shakes her head. "I hope not! We stake our reputation on the high quality of our cakes."

"What do you think it is, then?"

She presses her lips together as she looks at me. "Sophie, we need to talk."

"We should talk? But why?" My voice is suddenly breathless as my heart rate kicks up a level. Does she think I had something to do with her hurl fest? Did I inadvertently do something to make her sick?

Is she going to fire me?

Okay, maybe I'm being a touch drama queen-y right now. But seriously, how many people react rationally when they hear the words "we need to talk?"

Here's the thing about my job: it might not be super important, it might not be saving lives (that's Jason's department), it might not be making me squillions, but I love it. The Cozy Cottage Café is my home.

If I lost it, I'm not sure what I'd do.

"Is something wrong?" I ask nervously. "I know I've been late a couple of times in the last month, but it's really because of the bus I take and all that new construction down on David Street, you know the ones? What am I saying? *Of course* you know them. Everyone knows them. They're making everyone late. But I'm not usually late, you know that, and really, it was only by four or five minutes, six tops." Okay, seven easily, but I'm not trying to dig my grave here, people.

"It's okay, Sophie. Let's take a seat out in the café," Paige says by way of reply, which isn't a reply to my question at all, in my opinion.

Feeling increasingly desperate, I follow her through the door like I'm walking the line. With every step, I will her not to fire me. Even though rationally, other than the aforementioned lateness, I know I've done nothing wrong. It's like when you see a policeman, you instantly feel guilty, even if all you're doing is walking your family dog in the 'burbs down to the local store to buy a newspaper for your old-fashioned dad on a sunny Sunday morning.

But I digress.

We remove some chairs from on top of one of the tables and sit down. The room is dim, lit only by the light emanating from the kitchen on one side and the large street-facing windows on the other.

As I look at Paige, I hear Sean's voice in my head, telling me to wait for the other person to speak. Well, I blew that strategy out of the water back in the hallway. But now, as I sit in silence at the table, waiting for the guillotine to drop, I take Sean's advice and keep my mouth firmly shut.

Paige places her hands on the table, palms down. "First up, you're not being fired. You need to know we love you more than anything and the last thing we want is for you to leave us."

"Thank you," I gush. "I was worried for a moment there."

"And you know I'd never noticed you were late."

Great job, Sophie.

"Oh, it's only been a couple of times."

"It's fine, really. You're an excellent employee, Sophie, and our favorite barista."

"That's good to hear." I grin at her. "So, what's going on? Why do you need to talk to me?"

"Well, I've got some news."

It's the look on her face that makes me put two and two together. Her rush to the bathroom, her need to share something with me. It's got nothing to do with me at all!

"You're pregnant?" I chance.

She nods, a gorgeous grin busting out over her face. "I am. Twins."

"Twins?" I jump up and give her a shoulder hug across the table. It's awkward as all heck, but then hugging your boss is meant to be awkward, right? "Oh, that's wonderful news. Congrats! When are you due?"

"At the end of the year. We're having Christmas babies." She can't keep the excitement from her voice, and I don't blame her. One day, I want what she's got: a loving husband, a family, a place in the world. Right now, I'd settle for a decent date.

"I bet Josh is super happy."

"He did cartwheels in the back yard when I told him. Literally. Actual cartwheels," she says with a giggle. "And then he had a T-shirt made for me."

Josh is famous for his cheesy but adorable geek T-shirts with coffee puns. As he runs Ned's Coffee, a super successful roasting company who supplies our beans, it's kind of his thing, I guess.

"What does the T-shirt say?"

"It says, 'New human beans growing here,' and it's got an arrow pointing down to my belly with a picture of two beans in diapers."

"Cute!"

"I'm not quite game to wear it yet, especially as we've only just started telling people. But I wanted you to know. The morning sickness has been killing me."

Until this afternoon's dash, I'd not noticed Paige being anything other than the bubbly, sweet, and professional boss she is every day.

"Morning sickness sounds like it's misnamed, that's for sure."

"Totally. I get sick at all hours of the day. I threw up into Josh's shoe in the closet last night."

"Euw."

"I know, right? I didn't make it to the bathroom. I'm not sure he was overly impressed."

"He loves you, so he'll forgive you in a heartbeat. But I think that maybe that falls into the 'too much information' category for your employees." I shoot her a playful smile.

She lets out a laugh as she stands up and places the chair back upside down on the table, and I do the same. "I guess it is. Come out to the kitchen. Bailey and I have something else we need to talk to you about. Nothing bad," she adds hurriedly.

"Good to know. By now, you must know my imagination can run wild."

In the kitchen, Bailey's doing an inventory check in the refrigerator when Paige calls her out. She looks at us both standing by the counter and says, "Oh, it's time for the chat?"

"Sure is. I just told Sophie about these mini-cakes I'm baking in my belly."

"Isn't it exciting?" Bailey says with a huge smile on her beautiful face as she joins us.

"I had no idea," I reply honestly.

Bailey pats Paige on the back. "She's hidden it well. Now, Paige being pregnant is the reason we need to talk to you."

"You want me to take on some more shifts? Not cooking. I warn you; I can burn water. And I'm not just saying that. Mom asked me to boil some water to steam the beans a couple weeks back and I burned the pot. True story."

Bailey laughs. "Best we not ask Sophie to do any cooking then, Paige."

"Good job we didn't have that in mind."

"You know we think you're great, right, Sophie?" Bailey says.

"I didn't, but it's good to hear," I reply, which isn't strictly speaking true. My two bosses are such lovely people, they're always telling me how good I am at making coffee and how much they like working with me. I'm playing humble, lapping it up. Do not judge me. I'm on a low ebb and I need this.

"Well, we do," Paige says, "plus we know you have a finance degree, which might come in handy."

My interest is more than piqued. "For what, exactly?"

Paige glances at Bailey, who pulls out a fresh pink T-shirt with the words "Cozy Cottage High Tea" written in looping text across the chest.

"Cute shirt! Is that part of the new High Tea uniform? Did you want me to do some shifts there? Because I'd be happy to. I love it at High Tea."

"Here's the thing," Paige begins. "I've been having a tough time of it with this pregnancy, and on doctor's advice, Josh and I have decided I should take a step back for a while."

"So, with Paige having to be out of the picture, we wanted to ask you if you would like to be the weekend manager at Cozy Cottage High Tea," Bailey says.

"Excuse me? You want me to manage High Tea at the weekends?"

They both nod.

"But . . . that's the busiest time."

They both nod again, although it takes my brain a moment to catch up. "Seriously?" My voice is squeaking like a tiny mouse, high on helium now. "As in not just make coffee, but do managerial things like—" I wrack my brain for what managerial things might look like, but in my shocked state all I come up with is, "telling people what to do?"

More nods, this time accompanied by amused smiles at my obvious inability to fully comprehend what they're offering me.

"As in be the manager, as in be responsible for the business's profitability? As in be the *boss*?"

Bailey laughs. "Yes! Until Paige is back on her feet."

"After these babies are born," she adds.

"Sophie, your background combined with your love of the Cozy Cottage will be a total asset. I really hope you say yes." She glances at Paige. "*We* really hope you'll say yes."

My mind ticks over. Managing High Tea would be a dream job for me. Still the Cozy Cottage, but new and exciting.

Not only that, but Sean and my sisters might even see it as career-worthy for me. Perhaps they'd even drop the intern idea?

Paige bites her lip, her eyes bright. "Are you up for it? Because you have *so* got to be, Sophie. We don't trust anyone else to take care of High Tea the way we know you will."

"We would give you a pay raise, of course, and I'll help you transition," Bailey adds.

When I don't reply immediately, Paige says, "You don't need to give us an answer right now, Sophie. Take your time, think about it, talk it over with your family."

"Yes, we'll give you a full five minutes, right, Paige?" Bailey says with a smirk.

Excitement rises inside me at the prospect of managing the gorgeous brick building next door, with its kitschy cute scones and finger sandwiches, popular with the female population of Auckland.

I know what I want. It feels like this chance has been handed to me when I needed it the most.

Put that in your pipe and smoke it, overbearing older siblings!

"Actually, I don't need five minutes," I say. "I don't even need one minute. I would love to be the weekend manager at Cozy Cottage High Tea."

Chapter 7

"That's amazing! Congrats, babe." Darcy gives me a warm hug, and I breathe in her grapefruit-y perfume. "You so deserve this chance."

"Yeah, and you're going to totally rock it, girl," Erin says as she takes Darcy's place, collecting me in another hug. "I'm so proud of you, Soph."

"Thanks," I reply with a surge of happiness. "Cute dress, by the way."

"One of my original designs," Erin replies. "When do you start?"

"Next weekend, I am officially running the place. Well, with Bailey for a while at least." Excitement and sheer, unadulterated terror fight for pole position inside. I'd say excitement wins, but probably only due to the Chardonnay I virtually inhaled when we arrived at Jojo's Karaoke Bar.

"You're going to have to give us a discount, right?" Darcy says.

"Oh, you have to!" Erin adds. "I can see it now: we'll meet for high tea every Saturday and then regroup for karaoke. Cake, wine, and song. Perfect."

"So, let me get this straight. What you're saying is I'm going to become super fat on all those cakes as well as a terrible singer? Geez, I'll have no problem finding guys to date then," I reply with a laugh.

I may be joking, but on the inside, I'm fit to burst with happiness. It's been virtually impossible to keep my promotion to myself all week, but I wanted to tell my friends in person, and our Saturday night karaoke is the perfect moment.

"Your family must be stoked," Darcy comments.

"Mom and Dad were super excited when I told them. Dad was his usual 'you're my girl, of course you're a success,' and I think Mom used even more Irish-isms than ever before in her excitement."

When she gets like that, my brother and sisters call it "Mom Going Paddy." And go full force, no holds barred Paddy she sure did.

"I bet it was Irish-tastic," Darcy says.

"Could you even understand her?" Erin asks with a laugh. "When she gets going, she makes my head spin. In a good way, of course."

"Barely!" I reply with a laugh. "She even went so far as to label Paige and Bailey 'eejits' for not seeing my management potential up until now."

"Eejits?" Darcy questions.

"It means 'fool,'" I explain. "Everyone from the butcher who gave her a pork shoulder instead of a pork belly one time to the traffic warden who issued her with a parking ticket when she parallel parked over three angle parking spaces has been labeled an eejit at one time or another."

"Your mom is the bomb," Darcy says.

"I don't know about that, but I've got to admit, it felt great to make my parents proud. It's a feeling I've not had for a while now."

"Of course they're proud of you!" Erin rubs my arm.

"How about Sean and your sisters?" Darcy asks. "What did they think?"

As my BFFs, Erin and Darcy know all about the career interventions my siblings go in for. My excitement dims. "I've, ah, not told them yet. I made Mom and Dad swear on Granny's Bible that they wouldn't breathe a word of this to them, either. I want the chance to tell them in my own time."

Erin's face lights up. "This can be one of those deeply satisfying 'in your face' moments you see in movies. Like in *Pretty Woman* when she goes back to that store and tells them what a big mistake it was not to serve her. That was the best scene in the movie." She gets a faraway look in her eyes. "Or when *I* finally get my big break as a fashion designer and get to leave the world of self-satisfied sports pros behind."

Erin works in sponsorship for the Auckland City Hawks rugby team, which is not her dream job, although she's good at it. She'd rather spend her time creating designs for people of limited stature, like herself. (We never use the word "short.")

I shrug. "I don't know. I thought so to begin with, but now I'm not sure they'll see Weekend Manager at Cozy Cottage High Tea as nearly 'career' enough. And it's only for two days a week. Their newest intervention is for me to become an intern at one of their companies."

"Seriously? An intern?" Darcy's mouth drops open. "Aren't internships unpaid?"

I let out a puff of air as I press my lips into a line. "Yup."

Darcy's eyes are wide. "What about that little thing called money?"

"They suggested I move back home."

"Move back *home*?" Erin guffaws as Darcy scoffs, "What?!"

"Are they serious with this? You're *twenty-five*," Erin says.

"Exactly," Darcy agrees.

I shrug. "I get it. They're looking out for their little sister, that's all. They've got their lives all worked out and they want to help me, too."

Erin scrunches up her nose. "It sounds like you're considering it."

"I'm not," I reply firmly. "It's just—" What is it? They have a point? I should be doing more with my life? I didn't get myself a degree to be a barista all my life? I let out a huff. "I guess they've made me think, that's all."

"But now you have the High Tea thing." Erin beams at me.

"Exactly. Now I'm a manager, and I'm going to tell them I'm staying put."

"Good," Darcy says with a firm nod. "Because if you've got to leave your apartment, it would mean giving up the opportunity to catch Jason in just a towel each morning." Her face breaks into a smirk as she waggles her eyebrows at me.

I guffaw. "Darcy! I don't wait around to see that."

"Oh, you *should* wait around to see that, babe. That boy may act like he's God's gift to us women, but he most certainly has got the goods."

Erin nods. "It's true. He does. We've noticed."

"Got the goods?" I let out a light laugh. "Whether Jas has 'got the goods' or not as you so delightfully put it, how exactly did we go from talking about my exciting new job to how hot my roommate is in just a towel?" I shake my head at my friends.

Sure, I may have seen him in nothing but a towel once or twice, but it was totally by accident, even if he does have the kind of sculpted abs and broad shoulders that make many women swoon. He doesn't have that effect on me. He's just . . . Jason. I guess I'm simply impervious to his charms.

"It's all linked," Darcy says with a shrug. "Look, you don't need one of their crummy no-pay internships. You're running a successful high tea business now."

"At weekends," I add.

Darcy's grin is wide. "Weekend now, total world domination next."

"This calls for champagne," Erin announces. "Gosh, I've always wanted to say that," she adds with a giggle.

"Awesome idea, babe. I'll go get us some from the bar. Cristal okay with you all?" Darcy stands, her purse in hand.

"*Cristal?*" I sputter. "Do you have a money tree we don't know about these days, Darce?"

"I wish. I'm just messing with you. I'll get our regular cheap local version, but we can pretend it's Cristal, right?" She throws us a wink as she turns to leave. "BRB."

"You're going to have to sing something like *We are the Champions* or *Celebration* tonight, Soph," Erin says while Darcy makes her way to the bar.

"How about we choose a song recorded *after* we were born?"

"Are you saying my music taste isn't up to date? Sophie McCarthy, I am shocked." Erin's look of mock-offense has my happiness bubbling up inside once more.

"Pass me the catalog. I'll check it out."

Erin hands me the catalog, and I run my finger down the list of songs, looking for something fun and appropriately celebratory to sing. Most of the songs I find are about falling in love or breaking up, of course, but there are a few contenders in my somewhat narrow voice range.

Concentrating on the list, I'm startled by something plunked down on the table in front of me. I look up from the catalog at a bottle of champagne. The real stuff, not the sparkling wine plonk Darcy promised to get.

I shoot Darcy a questioning gaze. "You got us a bottle of Moët?"

She takes her seat at the table opposite me. "I didn't get us anything." She looks to the side and I follow her line of sight. Jason is approaching the table, champagne flutes held upside down by their stems in his hands. He's trailed by Ski Jump Nose—really, I should find out this girl's name—who's looking even prettier tonight with her blonde hair swept up in a high ponytail, her nose extra ski jump-y. If that's a thing.

"Jas? What are you doing here?" I say as I stand to greet him.

He pecks me on the cheek then places the glasses next to the bottle of champagne. "What are you talking about, McCarthy? You know how much I love karaoke."

I burst into laughter. "Jas, you hate karaoke."

"Yeah, okay. You got me. But I wanted to be here to celebrate your big news with my girls."

"*Your* girls?" Darcy, Erin, and I say in surprised unison as we gawp at him. He might have the goods hiding under that navy V-neck of his, but we're not his girls.

He shoots us a cheeky smirk. "Sure, why not? I've always seen myself as the kindly father of the group."

"You're nineteen months older than me, Jason. Nineteen months," I reply.

He puts his hand on my shoulder. "But, Sophie, those are a vital nineteen months. Vital."

I shake my head at him. With Jason still studying to be a doctor and his perpetual revolving door of girlfriends, his alleged maturity is just that; alleged. Mainly by the man himself.

"Maturity aside, it's so sweet of you to buy champagne," Erin says.

"It'll only be enough for a glass each. I'm still a poverty-stricken medical student, you know."

Ski Jump Nose prods him in the arm, and he seems to remember his manners. "Everyone, this is Megan Merson. We work together at the hospital."

Ski Jump Nose—sorry, *Megan*—waves at us, her pretty face breaking into the prettiest smile. Did I mention she's pretty? Like, most popular girl in school pretty. *So* Jason's type. "Hi, everyone. It's great to meet you all."

Jason points around the group. "This is Darcy, this is Erin, and this is the woman of the hour, Sophie."

"The woman of the hour? I think she should at least get a week, don't you, Soph?" Darcy says as Jason and Megan take their seats.

"Oh, totally," Erin echoes. "You need this."

Erin's right. I *do* need this. Getting this promotion has given me a new focus, a new lease on life, as Mom put it, in between calling me "*dote*," "*a leanbh*," "*a stór*," and a bunch of other Irish-isms when she went Paddy on me.

"Oh. We're missing a glass. I must have counted wrong," Jason says.

Darcy quirks an eyebrow. "You don't do math in med school?"

I hop up from my chair. "I'll get us another glass." I make my way over to the bar and wait patiently for the barman to finish serving the woman next to me.

"You're going to have to explain something to me, McCarthy." I turn to look at Jason, who has materialized at my side.

"What's that?"

"What exactly is high tea? Is it drinking tea while you sit on a highchair like a baby? Or something you might have done in college, if you get what I mean."

"You know this. You asked me when I first started working there. Remember?"

"Tell me again. I forget things." He taps the side of his head. "My brain is full of important medical information that saves lives, remember?"

"It's elegant sandwiches, little scones with jam and cream, slices of yumminess, all served with pots of tea."

"Sounds like snacks on steroids for the truly hungry."

"I guess it is. So, Megan seems nice," I lead.

"She's great."

"Is this the second date?"

"Second or third."

"Oh, this is serious!"

"You know me, McCarthy; I don't do serious."

"I can't remember the last time a girl lasted more than a week or two."

He grabs the barman's attention and asks for another champagne flute. "What have you told the McCarthy Mafia about the new job?"

Yup, complete change of subject. That's our Jason. He'll remain a commitment-phobe to the bitter end.

"Mom and Dad have been super excited about it, but Sean and my sisters? I'm not sure they'll see it as much of a promotion. Which I guess it's not, really. I mean, I'm only in charge at the weekends. I'm still 'only a barista' during the week." I use air quotes. My belly twists at the mere thought of sharing my news with my siblings.

"What's your gut telling you?"

"Right now, it's telling me to drink a glass of champagne to get some Dutch courage to sing."

He laughs, his dark eyes dancing. "Well in that case, we'd better get back to the table."

We make our way back to the others when he puts his hand on my arm and says, "Do me a favor, okay, McCarthy?"

"What?" I turn to look at him and notice how serious his face suddenly looks.

"Listen to what your gut tells you. It's never wrong."

"Is that your medical opinion, Almost-Doctor Christie?"

"It is. Now that'll be $150, thank you, miss."

I roll my eyes at him as I take my seat back at the table.

"The final piece of the puzzle." Jason brandishes the glass as he sits down next to Megan.

"Have you two come to sing?" Erin asks Jason and Megan hopefully as Jason shares the contents of the bottle between the five champagne flutes.

"That would be a hard no from me," Jason responds. "You're going to sing though, aren't you, Meg?"

"Oh, I love to sing," Megan gushes. "My whole family is musical. I grew up singing and playing the piano. We were in a band called The Mersons. You might have heard of us? We were kind of like New Zealand's answer to the Von Trapps. You know, from *The Sound of Music*."

"I didn't know Auckland had been occupied by the Nazis," Darcy quips.

"Oh, not that part. Just the family singing part," Megan clarifies for us unnecessarily, and I shoot Darcy a "be nice" glare.

"What?" she mouths at me, doing an extremely poor job of feigning innocence.

The thing is, Jason brings a series of random women to our get-togethers. They're all sweet, nice girls, pretty much cookie cutters of one another. We learned early on not to get attached to any of them because almost as soon as they're on the scene, they're off it again, and we're onto the next version of Megan before you can say "whiplash." Really, I think the longest a girl has lasted with Jason has been a month. Look "serial monogamist" up in the dictionary and you'll find a photo of Jason Christie, wearing that adorable smile of his that sets so many unsuspecting victims' hearts racing.

True story.

Jason raises his glass in a toast. "To Sophie and her brilliant new career."

"To Sophie and her brilliant new career," everyone echoes, and I beam at them as I take a sip of my champagne.

"Oh, that's so good," Darcy comments. "Much better than our usual."

"That's because our usual sits way at the other end of the scale," Erin comments.

"It tickles my nose," I say as I rub it. "It's so nice of you, Jas. Thank you."

"You're super generous, Jason. Sophie's *so* lucky to have you," Darcy says with a cheeky grin.

"You know what, Darce? I think I'm the lucky one. Sophie's quite the catch," Jason says in a mock Sean Connery as James Bond accent. It's his go-to accent of choice, and it's poor at best.

"Oh, the guy who gets Sophie will be very lucky," Erin says. "And speaking of which, we've got some vetting to do before the first big date, right, Soph?"

"Yes, although I need to meet him to see if I want to take it to the next level first." My heart rate kicks up a notch at the thought of dating Oliver, the "good guy" Paige wants to set me up with.

"Well, duh," Erin says.

"What's this?" Jason asks. "You've got a date already?"

"Maybe. We need to vet him, though. Make sure he's one of the good ones." I take another sip of my champagne, the bubbles tickling my nose once more. "I got some tips at the café this week from Cassie on how to do it. Apparently, she had an entire dossier on the guy she chose. She left no stone unturned."

"We don't want any wolves in sheep's clothing," Darcy says. "I've dated guys like that. They look like normal, fully functioning men on the outside, but on the inside? Raving freaking lunatics."

Jason's eyes are dancing when he questions, "Lunatics? What did they do, escape from the local asylum just so that they could date you?"

"That's right," Darcy confirms, her face impassive.

"Ok*aaay*," Jason replies with a sarcastic lilt. "So, back to the *real* world. Who is this guy, Soph?"

"His name is Oliver Price. He worked with Paige at A.G.D. I've done some detective work and found out a few things about him, and so far, he seems pretty good. Cute, smart, a bit of an action man."

"An action man sounds good. He'll have a great body, all buff and athletic. Think G.I. Joe," Erin says.

"But hopefully not made of plastic," Darcy adds.

"You're on fire tonight, Darce," I say.

"But why are you stalking this guy? Why don't you just ask him out?" Megan asks.

"Because of the pact," Erin explains. "We three girls have made a pact not to date jerks anymore. We have a long history, you see."

"A long and bitter history," I confirm.

"Oh, we've all been there," Megan replies. "That's why I'm glad I'm dating a nice guy like Jason now."

"Yeah," I reply with a not altogether honest head nod at the same time as Erin says, "True," and Darcy echoes, "Totally."

Although we all know Jason is far from boyfriend material, there's no need to upset the girl.

A swift change of topic is needed. "We've got to agree how we're going to do the No More Bad Dates Pact."

"Rules. That's what we need," Darcy begins. "There needs to be an initial contact phase, after which we need to vet the guys to see if the girl who wants to date him has missed any red flags."

Jason's lips quirk into a smile. "An initial contact phase? Is that what normal people would call a first date?"

"Well, yes, but it's not," I reply.

"Exactly. It can't be a date. It's just a 'getting to know you' thing," Erin says. "That way it's not an official date."

Jason leans back in his chair. "This all sounds way too technical for me."

"I'll put some rules together and email them to you both," Darcy offers.

"Don't forget me," Jason says to enquiring looks from my female friends. I'd neglected to tell them Jason was lending an "expert" hand in our pact, as he'd put it.

"You're part of the pact?" Erin questions as her eyes dart to Megan. "It's for us singletons, you know."

"Oh, I know," he replies, his arm hanging off the back of Megan's chair. "Think of me as a guest judge on *American Idol*. I'm full of expert advice and strong mentoring capabilities."

I laugh. "You really lack confidence, you know that, Christie?"

"Are you going to be an 'expert' for all of us, or just your room-mate?" Darcy asks.

"I want to share the love around, so I'm offering my services to the whole group, if you want them," Jason replies.

Darcy's jaw clenches. "When I finally meet a guy who warrants vetting, I'll let you know."

"You will, Darce. Not all guys are slimeballs." This from Erin.

Darcy has dated some real doozies in the past. "Slimeball" is probably the nicest thing Erin could say about any one of them.

I clap my hands. "That's settled then. I'll text you all a date and time for the vetting once I've met this guy, and you can interrogate him."

Jason raises his glass. "To interrogating the living crap out of the unsuspecting male population."

We all clink glasses.

"I only hope he's not scared off by you all," I say.

"And if he is, he wasn't your man, anyway," Erin says.

I pick the song catalog up again. "I think I've found the perfect song for tonight."

"What is it?" Jason asks.

"*On Top of the World*." I grin at my friends, confident in my choice of happy song to celebrate my success.

"Imagine Dragons? I *love* that song," Jason exclaims.

"I know you do. But I can't say you will once I'm done slaughtering it." I laugh self-deprecatingly, despite my friend's protestations.

I punch the song number into the device on the table and it immediately flashes up the number three. Third in line. Time to lube the vocal cords with the rest of my champagne.

"I'm going to sing, too," Megan announces.

"Good for you! Are you a karaoke queen?" Erin asks.

"The Von Trapps, remember? We sang a lot as kids," she replies.

"Do re mi." Darcy shoots me a smile.

"Fa so la ti do," Megan finishes in a sing-song-y voice, and then to our astonishment continues to sing, "Doe, a deer, a female deer, ray, a drop of golden sun." She grins at us. "I love *The Sound of Music*."

"We can tell," Darcy says.

"You've got a lovely voice," Erin, ever the sweetheart, says. "I'm looking forward to hearing you sing."

"Well, you won't have to wait too long. She's number two on the lineup, and the first group's about to begin," Jason says as he gestures toward the stage.

Three women about our age are looking about as nervous as a bunch of deer during hunting season as they wait for the music to kick in.

"Tell me more about this band of yours. Do you still play?" Erin asks Megan.

"Oh, yes. Well, not my parents anymore, but my three brothers and I have a band. We play the classics, you know, seventies stuff. I'm the lead singer."

"Awesome! I love the music of the seventies. I bet you're amazing." Erin is clearly impressed.

The opening bars of "Never Gonna Give You Up" resound around the room, putting an end to Erin and Megan's buddy-buddy get to know each other session.

"Rick Astley. Now there's some karaoke gold, right there," Jason says as the girls on the stage begin to sing the opening line with shaky, uncertain voices. After they butcher the first chorus—and I'm not complaining here; these girls make me look like freaking Adele —they relax into it, and with the crowd's support, manage to pull the whole song off with their pride intact. Well, mostly.

That's the awesome thing about Jojo's Karaoke. No matter how bad you are, people support you when you're up there on the stage. Of course, they may never invite you back, but that's another thing.

One of the waiters announces the next in line, and Megan pops up from her seat. "A good luck kiss, please." She pats the side of her cheek, and to my surprise, Jason reaches up from his seat and kisses her.

"You're very obedient," I comment once Megan is out of earshot. "You must really like this girl."

"He's just being a good doggie, aren't you, Jas?" Darcy teases with a smirk.

"Megan's great," he replies, clearly ignoring Darcy's gentle jibe.

"I bet she's going to sing this song beautifully, too," Erin says.

We hear the opening bars to "Wrecking Ball" followed by Megan's singing, her voice strong and rich and beautiful. Seriously, she sounds like Miley Cyrus, only better, because she's here in the room with us—and not writhing around naked on an oversized metal ball as she licks a mallet.

Thank God.

We sit and listen, spellbound, right to her very last note, after which the crowd bursts into spontaneous, enthusiastic, *genuine* applause. Megan gives a bashful and totally endearing curtsey before returning to our table where we all congratulate her on her stellar performance.

"You seriously undersold your talents with that Von Trapp thing," I say with a shake of my head.

How am I going to follow *that*?

I don't even have time to think about it before my name is called and I'm the one up on the tiny stage, the lights shining bright in my eyes. I grab the microphone as the first bars of "On Top of the World" play, and say, "For what you're about to hear, I am truly, truly sorry."

And then I launch into the song, thankful it's low enough that my voice is disguised, until someone shouts, "We can't hear you!" I respond with a louder voice, and it's then that I remember how much I love this. So what if Megan sounds incredible? I come here almost every Saturday night to do this and I'm going to give it my all. I may sound like a pack of cats fighting to get out of a box, but you know what? I have passion, willing, and at least two glasses of wine inside me.

Just like my new job as Weekend Manager of Cozy Cottage High Tea, and my Initial Contact with Oliver "the good guy" Price, I may not be perfect, but I've totally got this.

Chapter 8

When you're a McCarthy, Sundays mean it's time for another Mandatory McCarthy Meal, and this Sunday is no exception. As I'll be taking over High Tea as of next weekend, this will be my last Sunday family lunch for the foreseeable future, and I'm both excited and sad about it.

Mom has served up her delicious, hearty lamb stew with potato mash—always potatoes, we're not Irish for nothing, you know—designed to "put hairs on your chest," as Dad likes to say. Not that putting hairs on my chest is a personal goal, of course.

I've devoured it in record time then sit and wait for a break in the conversation to share my High Tea news with Sean, Abigail, Fiona, and Caitlin. Mom keeps winking at me conspiratorially across the table, and I've caught Dad shooting me glowing looks since we sat down.

"Subtle" is not a word often used in describing Siobhan and Patrick McCarthy.

I'm not expecting my siblings to be quite as positive about it all.

"But you see, Caitlin, therein lies the rub," Sean says, using one of his Shakespearean expressions.

"No, Sean, there's no 'rub' here. Those political activists need to stay home and do something useful with their time," Fiona says.

"You're missing the point," Sean replies.

"Err, excuse me, everyone," I begin. All eyes at the table turn to me. Well, only one of Mom's eyes, the other one is too busy winking at me, knowing full well what I'm about to announce.

"What is it, *a stór*? Do you have something important to tell everyone at the table? Perhaps you have some *big news*?" Mom leads with as much delicacy as a habanero chili.

"Yes, thanks, Mom," I mutter.

Fiona's eyes light up. "Ooh, is this about the internship, Sophie? Will we be seeing you grace the halls of McCarthy & McCarthy shortly?"

"No, no. Fiona, she won't choose a stuffy old law practice over working in an exciting, dynamic online store like Baby-ness," Caitlin says. "Will you, Sophie?"

I open my mouth to reply when Sean, predictably, jumps in with his two cents worth. Or should that be two shillings worth? I have no clue what money they used in Shakespearean England. "Granted, your business is doing well, but it's a startup, Caitlin. McCarthy & McCarthy is an established legal practice with two of us spearheading its success. Methink'st Sophie would be a fool not to choose us."

"All right, you three," Dad says, and not a moment too soon. "You can 'methink'st' what you like after Sophie's made her announcement, Sean." He smiles down the table at me. "Now. What did you want to tell us all, love?"

I shoot him a grateful look before I clear my throat. "You're right, I have made a decision about the internships." I can feel a smile teasing at the edges of my mouth as I think about my new responsibilities at Cozy Cottage High Tea. "As of next weekend, I won't be able to attend this lunch. I have accepted the job of Weekend Manager at Cozy Cottage High Tea. It's temporary, but it's a start." I look around the table at my siblings. They are all watching me closely, waiting for me to say more. Do I need to repeat myself?

Mom claps her hands together and beams around the table. "Isn't that quite something? Our little Sophie; a manager!"

When no one says anything further, Dad adds, "Well, aren't you going to congratulate your sister?"

"Yes, of course. Well done," Abigail says at the same time as Fiona, Sean, and Caitlin all murmur their clearly heartfelt congratulations, too.

"If anyone wants to eat a lot of cake, they know where to go. Our Sophie will make sure they're properly fed and watered," Dad says with a warm smile.

I return his smile and say, "Thanks, Dad."

"Just a minute. Clarify something for me if you will, Sophie." Sean's knitted his brow together so tightly he's sporting a bushy mono-brow. It's not a good look. "You're going from having a full-time job as a barista in a café to managing their high tea business two days a week? And it's only temporary? Why?"

"Paige, one of my bosses, has got bad morning sickness," I reply.

"Hyperemesis Gravidarum," Caitlin says with a sage nod. "It's basically Latin for throwing your guts up day in, day out."

"Delightful," Sean says. "Thanks for that, Caitlin."

"Well, whatever it's called, she's not been well and needs to take some time out." A surge of pride hits me as I add, "They said they trust me and don't want anyone else to manage the place."

"So, it's a temporary position until this boss of yours has stopped throwing up so much?" Sean asks.

"She's said she won't be back until after the babies are born," I reply.

Caitlin pulls a face. "Ooh, twins. That'll be a shock."

Undeterred, Sean continues, "And when this woman with the Latin morning sickness—"

"Hyperemesis Gravidarum," Caitlin repeats.

"Yes, that. When she returns to work, you'll go back to being just a barista in the café again?" Sean asks.

And there it is: *just a barista.* I do my best to ignore the twist in my belly at his words.

"Oh, come on, Sean. Be fair. She does a very good job of it."
Abigail shoots me what I think is intended to be an encouraging
smile, but it only adds to a feeling of inadequacy that has begun to
spread across my chest.

"What about the internships we offered you?" he asks. "They
don't pay the way this temporary weekend job of yours does, but at
least there's scope for promotion, a future."

Each and every one of my siblings lean in, ready to hear my
decision.

I curl my toes inside my shoes. "I'm, ah, not going to take either
of them. But thank you for offering them to me."

"Sophie, I am so disappointed in your decision," Caitlin says.

Sean and Fiona immediately sit back in their seats, muttering
things like, "We should have seen *that* coming," and, "these Millen-
nials have always got to go for the shiny new thing, and, "Methink'st
she doth make a grave mistake." The last statement was from Sean,
clearly.

"Look, I know I've disappointed you all, but this has got to be
my decision," When no one says anything, I add, "It's my life," just
in case any of them had failed to notice this minor, insignificant fact.

"Sophie, remember. We know what we are, but know not what
we may be," Sean says with a wise nod of the head.

I crumple my forehead as I try to work out what the heck he's
talking about.

"Must you always quote The Bard, Sean? It can get old,"
Abigail says.

"I think it's just lovely that you're all fighting over your sister,"
Mom states. "I've always said it: there's nothing like family. And,
love?" She looks in my direction.

"Yes, Mom?" She's about to Go Paddy on me.

"You've got to do your own growing, no matter how tall your
father is."

It's an old Irish saying that says no matter how successful others
in my family are, I need to find my own success. I can't help but
smile at Dad. He winks at me, a big grin on his face.

"Yes, Mom."

Caitlin sits up straighter in her chair and announces, "I've got an idea. Something I think we can all agree to. Sophie can give this High Tea thing a shot while her boss is suffering, the poor woman, and when she's back, we can reassess things."

I don't like the sound of "reassess things." It sounds an awful lot like "tell Sophie to take one of our crummy internships" to me.

"Brilliant idea, Caitlin," Sean replies eagerly.

"I agree," Fiona adds. "What do you think, Sophie?"

"Oh, err, I guess," I reply uncertainly.

"By doing it this way, you can keep your options open. How many weeks is she?" Caitlin asks.

I shrug. "I think she's fifteen or something?"

"So, assuming she's not coming back to work straight away after she gives birth, that gives you, say, eight months to make this work."

Part of me knows Caitlin's suggestion makes sense. I haven't talked to Bailey and Paige about what happens once Paige is back. Do I go back to being a barista? If I do, will that then be enough for me?

I pull my lips into a thin line and nod.

Caitlin sits back in her chair and exclaims, "Excellent. It looks like we have a solution."

Eight months.

Eight months to live my dream of managing High Tea.

Eight months to prove to my bosses that I'm too good to lose.

———

ONCE I'M SAFELY BACK at my apartment later that day, my phone beeps with a new email. It's from the very-organized and precise Darcy and *No More Bad Dates Pact Rules of Engagement* is the email heading. This is it, the details of how we plan to help one another vet these potential dates of ours.

I'm the first to take the plunge, and it's starting to freak me out.

I get myself comfortable on my bed and open the email.

Remember ladies (and Jason), this is war. Approach all potential targets with extreme care. Guys are the enemy, until proven otherwise.

Enemy? Potential targets? I shake my head, my insides tightening. This is sounding less and less like dating to me and more like out and out warfare.

I read on.

Recommended Rules of Engagement:

Acceptable ways to meet targets include (but are not limited to) set-ups, friends of friends, work colleagues (not recommended. I'm thinking of you, Sophie).

I press my lips together as I involuntarily take an unpleasant walk down memory lane. What I've learned about work romances is that hot barista from Sweden plus Sophie "I'll fall for anything you say" McCarthy equals heartbreak. Some may say it was inevitable, considering Sven, the guy in question, was only in Auckland on a temporary visa, but when he told me he wanted to take me home to meet his mom and sample her famous meatballs, I was fool enough to believe him. I know, I know. Gullible, trustworthy, a total idiot. Take your pick.

Steps:

- *Initial Contact. First official meeting. Initial Contacts are to occur over tea, coffee, or other non-alcoholic beverages only. Must be in public. Coffee houses recommended. Liquor strictly banned. Physical contact discouraged.*
- *Target must agree to the next step, otherwise, eliminate.*

Eliminate? Good Lord, Darcy. She's definitely channeling her inner Hermione with this whole thing. I feel sorry for her boss.

- *Vetting Process by other team members to determine jerk status. Dater's choice to be present. If, and only if, no red flags are uncovered, move on to the next step with caution. Remember, this is war.*

Yup, Darcy, I think we've all got that by now.

- *Second Official Meeting (can be referred to as "First Date"). Can include meals, drinks, walks, etc. Note: target can turn jerk at any time. Be vigilant!*

- *Ongoing Meetings: Eliminate if jerk-like behavior is detected. If not, you are free to date.*

I lower my phone onto the bed covers beside me. After reading the Pact rules, the idea of meeting this guy Paige has set me up with feels about as appealing as planting my face in a bucket of angry bees.

It can't be that bad. Can it? Sure, I've dated some jerks in the past, and sure, my ability to spot them has not exactly been what anyone would call "stellar." But the No More Bad Dates Pact Rules of Engagement are enough to put anyone off dating ever again!

I let out a sigh as I lean my head back against my padded head-board. I've committed to this, so it's going to work.

It's just got to.

Chapter 9

It's Monday morning and I'm psyching myself up to meet Oliver Price for my inaugural Initial Contact. Per the No More Bad Dates Pact Rules of Engagement, we've agreed to meet at a coffee house near his work. It's called Alessandro's, a place I've not been to before, and as I push my way through the heavy glass door, I'm immediately struck by the aroma of freshly brewed coffee and chatter from the busy café.

As I scan the room for the guy who fits the description Paige gave me—okay, and the guy who looks like the person I've already spent hours stalking on social media—I try my best not to think of him as "the enemy." No matter what Darcy says, this is not war. This is a date, and he's just a guy, out to meet a girl, like everyone else.

So why do I feel like I'm about to walk across the freaking Somme right now?

I steel myself with a deep breath. It doesn't take long to spot him amidst the hubbub of the café. He looks like his photos, only better. He's sitting at a table for two, concentrating on something on his phone. I seize the moment to look him over. No, forget that. I don't just look him over, I drink him in. He's hot like Zac Efron meets

Gerard Butler, but I can tell he's also super tall, his long legs reaching way past the edge of the small table. As I look at him, I notice there's even a hint of Sheldon from *The Big Bang Theory* thrown in to geek him up a notch.

Seriously, how is this guy still single? As I walk over to his table, I say a little silent prayer I'm not about to find out.

I repeat *please don't be a jerk, please don't be a jerk* in my head with every step until I come to a nervous stop beside him, my throat dry with apprehension. "Oliver?"

He looks up at me, and his face breaks into a smile. Zac, Gerard, and Sheldon. A weirdly perfect combination, which on Oliver Price, just simply works. "You've got to be Sophie."

"Sure am."

He pushes himself up, his chair making a screeching noise across the tiled floor as he stands to his full height. And he is *tall*. Like basketball player tall. Tall and totally cute. "It's great to meet you." He leans down and kisses me on the cheek, and I feel a flush begin to bloom where his lips touched.

"You, too." I smile at him like a star-struck teenage girl. No pygmy at five foot eight, this guy makes me feel small and feminine. And I kind of like it. I know it's old fashioned, but it's nice to feel small and feminine for a change—and yes, I know I've set the women's movement back about fifty years by thinking it.

"I hope you don't mind, but I checked with Paige to see how you have your coffee." He gestures at what looks like a latte on the table. "Double shot skinny latte, right?"

Happiness spreads through me as I peer up at him. "Thank you so much, Oliver. That's so sweet."

He shrugs, looking embarrassed. It's completely adorable. "I guess I wanted to make a good impression. Paige said some really great things about you."

"She said some really great things about you, too."

We stand by the table, smiling our shy smiles at one another like a couple of goofballs before Oliver says, "Did you want to sit down?"

"Oh, yes!" I let out a light laugh as we both sit at the table.

"Try the coffee," he says.

I pick the coffee cup up and raise it to my lips. Oliver watches me closely, so close that I lower the cup and say, "What?"

"Oh, sorry. I guess I was staring, right?"

"Kind of, yeah."

He gives a self-effacing shrug. "It's just, Paige said you're a brilliant barista, and I guess I'm nervous the coffee won't be up to your usual standard."

Could this guy get any sweeter?

"I'm sure it'll be great." I take a sip before he can say another word. "It's excellent," I declare, even though it's not. But hey, this guy is cute, he's done a really sweet thing for me, and right now, my hopes are so high they're in fear of getting vertigo.

"Awesome." He grins at me some more, and things zing around inside of me.

"So, tell me about yourself, Oliver."

"Sure. I guess you know where I work because of Paige. I've been at A.G.D. for about six years now, ever since I graduated, in fact. I guess I'm one of those types of people who joined the graduate program and liked it so much they stayed."

I've not heard that's a type exactly, but I go with it. "You're in marketing, right?"

"Product marketing. Every time A.G.D. has a new product, me and my team put together marketing plans for it."

"And you love doing it?"

"I do. My goal is to run the team sometime soon then keep taking steps up the corporate ladder."

"A man of ambition, huh?"

My siblings will adore him.

He gives another one of those shy smiles that had me swooning before. "I've got goals, and I'm not afraid to go after them. How about you?"

I think of the Cozy Cottage. "Oh, I love what I do, too. In fact, I've just been promoted."

"Seriously? To what?"

"I'm the Weekend Manager at Cozy Cottage High Tea."

"High tea?"

I laugh. "It's probably more of a girl thing. It's where you sit around for hours on end and eat a lot of yummy things. Oh, and drink endless cups of tea. Or coffee."

"I could totally get on board with the eating thing, but the tea?" He scrunches up his face. "Not so much."

"I'm kind of the same, although if you tell my mom that, I'll be hung and quartered."

"She's that serious about tea?"

"She's Irish."

"Got it."

"Anyway, I'm training myself to drink it. And you know what? Earl Grey is really nice, and there's this one called Lapsang Souchong that's smoky and interesting."

"Lapsang what?" A smile teases the edges of his mouth.

"Souchong," I repeat as I return his smile. "It's from the mountainous Wuyi region in the Chinese province of Fujian."

He leans back in his chair and studies my face. "You know your stuff."

I shrug. I'm enjoying this so much! "I try. There's a lot to learn about tea, and I guess I want to make sure I'm knowledgeable in front of the customers."

"I'm sure they'll all be dazzled by you," he replies, and warmth spreads across my chest.

Great work, Paige!

"Oh, I don't know about that." I take another sip of my average coffee, feeling embarrassed. "There's so much more to know. I haven't even started on herbals."

"Herbals aren't tea. They're nice smelling water."

I giggle. "And don't forget no caffeine."

"Exactly. What's the point?"

I grin at him, not quite believing this set-up is going so incredibly well. Oliver Price, where have you been all my dating life?

"Paige tells me you like to fish."

His face lights up. "I sure do."

My interest in fishing is less than zero, but listening to Oliver's enthusiasm and watching the way his face lights up, I think fishing has rapidly become my new favorite topic of conversation. At least with this guy.

Sometime later, our coffee cups empty, the alarm on my phone sounds, signaling our Initial Meeting should now be at an end. Although I could happily stay here with Oliver and talk for the rest of the day, I really can't go breaking the rules this early on. Darcy would definitely have something to say about it, and this is the first ever No More Bad Dates Initial Meeting. Standards need to be set. (Oh, no, I sound like Darcy.)

As we walk out of the café and onto the street, he looks at me from his lofty height and says, "This has been nice. Let's do it again sometime."

"I'd like that."

I know what I need to do next. I need to tell him about the No More Bad Dates Vetting Process, and my nerves are doing overtime. "I've got to ask you something really weird."

"Weird can be good."

"My friends and I have made a pact, and part of it is that any guy we want to date needs to meet the group first."

"That seems sensible enough. There are a lot of weirdos out there, you know."

Relieved, I let out a light laugh. "That's good. So, if we are to go out together again, you'd be fine to meet them?"

His smile beams down at me. "Dinner. My treat. We can meet them for a drink first."

I bite my lip as a grin busts out across my face. This is going to work! I've finally found a non-jerk, a great guy, and he wants to go out with me.

I can hardly wait for our first official date.

⸺

I DON'T HAVE to wait long until D-Day rolls around, the day Oliver faces my friends to be vetted within an inch of his life. So it really could be called V-Day for Vetting Day, but I'm pretty sure that means "Victory Day," and I'm not exactly feeling victorious. In fact, I'm about as nervous as a Real Housewife getting her first lip injections.

Call me crazy, but I made the call to exercise my "dater's choice to be present," per the Rules of Engagement. What that means in plain old English is that right now, I'm waiting with Darcy, Erin, and Jason, to interrogate Oliver.

I feel sorry for him. But then I think of Andrew Foster and the way he unceremoniously dumped me at Bailey's wedding and then moved straight on to the next girl without even a backward glance, and I know I absolutely do not have a choice in this. If I want to date, I need to take control. And that's what tonight is all about.

Jason leans back in his seat across the table from me. "I still can't believe this guy agreed to meet your friends before he's even been on a proper date with you. I would *never* do that."

"Why not?" Erin asks.

"Because it's insane, that's why."

"No, it's not," Darcy protests. "Vetting potential dates underpins our entire dating philosophy. Well, our *new* dating philosophy."

But Jason is like a dog with a juicy bone. "Think about it: you're set up on a blind date with a friend of a friend, and instead of getting to spend the date with that person, you meet a tribe of their friends who've come armed with a list of personal questions." He points at the notepad on the table in front of Erin. "Literally."

Darcy shrugs. "It's either that or no date, and he clearly wants to go out with your roommate."

"Well, I get that. Sophie's a total catch." He winks at me.

Indignant at his insinuation that I'm the opposite of a catch, I say, "I *am* a total catch."

Jason shrugs. "That's what I said. But you do need to do some serious work on your gaming skills."

"You want to talk about my gaming skills right now?" I ask.

"Remind me; have you ever beaten me at *Fortnite*?" Jason says.

I shake my head at him. "See? You're showing us exactly why this committee should be girls only."

Darcy crosses her arms. "Focus, Jason. Got it?"

He puts his hands up in the air in surrender. "Got it."

Darcy looks around the group. "Has everyone got their questions at the ready?"

"Yes," Erin replies as Jason says, "Questions?"

Erin shakes her head. "I texted them to you last night."

Jason picks his phone up off the table and begins to scroll through his messages. "I thought that was just you drunk texting random things to me."

Erin looks offended. "I never drunk text."

I clear my throat as Darcy and I share a look. Drunk texting has been Erin's "thing" for way too long. She breaks up with a guy and her resolve not to ever contact him again glides further and further down a slippery slope with her every sip of Chardonnay. Girls' karaoke night after one of Erin's breakups often requires one of us to wrestle her phone from her at the end of the night.

Erin holds her index finger up. "*One* time. And I really did think he was still into me."

"Honey, I don't want to sound harsh, but it's been maybe a few more times than once," I say.

Erin slumps back in her chair. "Twice then. But seriously guys, I've learned my lesson. Never again."

That's the other thing Erin does: declare she'll never drunk text again. Which of course lasts until the next time something goes wrong with a guy and she has that glass of Chardonnay. Really, she's a danger unto herself.

"Anyway, we're not here to talk about me and my failings with men, many as they may be. We're here for Sophie," Erin declares.

"Exactly. Jason, read your questions," Darcy instructs.

"And remember, we're not looking for H.E.A.s here, just H.F.N.s. Absolute perfection isn't required." As I remind them of the premise of the No More Bad Dates Pact, Darcy and Erin both nod.

Jason's face is creased up in confusion. "What *language* are you talking, McCarthy?"

"Seriously, Jason. Read your message!" Erin says with force.

"An H.F.N. stands for 'happy for now.' It means he might not be The One, but he's more than good enough for now," I explain.

Darcy quirks an eyebrow. "Kind of like you and all those nurses."

Jason lets out a laugh, his eyes dancing. "Some of them are trainee doctors like me, you know."

"It's so good to hear you don't discriminate," Darcy deadpans.

"Stop, you guys." My heart leaps into my mouth when I spot Oliver. He's standing next to the bar, scanning the room. Dressed in a white polo shirt and a pair of jeans, he looms tall over most of the people nearby, standing out like the mini-giant he is. "He's here."

"Where?" Erin's head whips around, making it as obvious as grass stains on white pants that she's looking for him. "Him? The super tall guy?"

"Yes, but don't make it so obvious," I say to her through my teeth.

"Wow. That guy's a dead ringer for Danny DeVito," Jason says.

I suppress a giggle as I stand up. Jason's being too annoying right now for me to give him the satisfaction of laughing at his joke.

I feel Jason's hand on my arm and look down to see him staring up at me, an earnest look on his face. "Soph? Is now a good time to point out once again that we are all here to vet the crap out of this guy, and he *agreed* to it?"

I pull my arm away and ignore him. I walk over to greet Oliver. His face lights up when he spots me, and he gives me a hug and kiss on the cheek in greeting. It's sweet, and I instantly feel bad for putting him through this whole vetting palaver. "Are you sure you're up for this?" I ask him, half hoping he'll choose to back out and he and I can make a run for it through the fire escape together.

"Of course. You're worth it." He smiles at me, and my belly does a little flip. "If I need to prove to you that I'm a decent guy before you'll let me take you to dinner, then I say bring it on."

I grin at him. "You're a total rock star."

We walk over to the table together, me feeling like I'm leading an oversized lamb to the slaughter, and him? Well, I'm not sure what he's thinking, but I'm more than glad he's here.

My friends all greet him, and we take our seats.

Darcy places her hands on the notebook in front of her. "First up, thank you for being here today, Oliver. We know this isn't what you might be expecting when you start seeing someone new, so we're really pleased you're up for it."

Oliver looks around the table. "Look, feel free to ask me anything you want. I'm an open book."

"Are you now?" Darcy says. "Let's get started then. Erin?"

Erin places her finger on the first line of her notepad and clears her throat. "How did your last relationship end and why?"

"She decided it was over. It was rough at the time. We'd been together for a while."

"How did it happen?" Erin persists.

"You want specifics?" Oliver asks and Erin nods. "She met someone else. She left me for him." The fleeting look of sadness on his face has my heart contracting for him. "As I said, it was a rough time for me."

"Oh, I'm sorry," Erin says, her brow creased in concern for him. "I know what that's like. It totally sucks."

"Okay, next question," Darcy says. "Jason?"

Jason reads his phone, looks up at Darcy, and says, "You seriously want me to ask him this?"

"That's the whole point," she hisses out of the corner of her mouth.

Jason shrugs. "Okay then." He looks up at Oliver. "Oliver, what do you do to express your feelings for someone you're dating?"

I press my lips together to stop a smile. I don't think I've ever heard the word "feelings" come out of Jason's mouth in my life. Well, other than "I'm feeling hungry," which he says frequently.

"Well," Oliver begins, "I guess I might simply tell her how I feel, but often I'll show her by cooking a delicious meal. I think food is a wonderful way to express your feelings for someone." He turns to me. "I like to cook."

"Good, because Sophie doesn't," Erin says.

I shoot her a look that tells her to shush it. He doesn't need to know my flaws just yet.

"You don't like to cook?" Oliver asks me, the look on his face telling me exactly how outlandish the concept is to him.

Reluctantly, not wanting to put this guy off—Zac Efron meets Gerard Butler with a touch of Sheldon, remember?—but not wanting to lie, either, I say, "I'm pretty good at toast, I guess."

"You are good at toast," Jason confirms. "I'm not boasting here, but I taught her all she knows. How to toast bread, how to butter toast, even how to smother it with peanut butter. She's quite the gourmet toast chef these days."

Oliver's eyebrows shoot up. "Did you two date?"

I laugh, perhaps a little too loudly. "No! Jason's my roommate. That's how he knows about my finely tuned skills with the afore-mentioned toast."

Oliver nods, his lips drawn into a thin line. "Good to know." His eyes dart to mine. "You don't cook, but you like to eat, right?"

"Oh, yes! I'm big on eating. I love food. *Love* it."

Do I sound a little too eager?

Oliver's lips twitch into a smile. "That's good to hear. I like food, too."

We share a smile, and I ignore a little voice inside my head that says, "doesn't pretty much everyone like food?"

"Next question's from me," Darcy begins. "If I were to ask your most recent ex about you, what would she say?"

Oliver's eyes widen. "Wow, you guys like to ask the tough questions, don't you?"

"Yes, Oliver, we do." Darcy's eyebrows knit together as she sizes him up.

"Okay. Well, the last girl I dated would probably say I'm a good guy, a good cook," he looks at me, "but that ultimately, we weren't right for one another. Hence why she took off with another guy."

Her pen poised over her notepad, Darcy says, "Can I get her to corroborate that?"

"Oh, come on!" Jason exclaims as he throws his hands in the air. "Can't you leave the guy with some small part of his dignity intact? He's answered a load of personal questions. Do you think you can leave the ex alone?"

Darcy glares at him. "See? I knew it would be a bad idea to have a guy in on the Vetting Committee. Particularly if that guy is Jason Christie."

"Thanks, man." Oliver fist bumps Jason across the table. "Look, I hope I've answered these questions the way you wanted me to. Right now, I'm only interested in knowing if I passed. Because if I have, I've booked a restaurant table at Chez Pierre for eight, and I'd really quite like to take Sophie there."

I smile and look at him through my lashes. As far as I'm concerned, Oliver has passed with flying colors. And anyway, Chez Pierre is a super fancy French restaurant my brother loves to brag about going to, a place I've never been able to afford. The chance to go to such a high-end and romantic place with Oliver makes me want this date even more.

Darcy flips her notepad cover over. "Oliver, if you can give us a few minutes, we'll let you know our verdict."

"Sure. I'll be over at the bar. After this, I think I deserve a beer."

"I think you do, too," Jason says.

Oliver gets up and shoots me a small smile before he leaves.

When he's out of earshot, I bite my lip and say, "So? What did you think?"

"Oh, he's great!" Erin declares instantly. "He's considerate and kind and cares about the women he dates. He gets the green light from me."

I turn to Darcy. "What did you think?"

"Well, although I'm not about to swoon over him like you two are," she raises her eyebrows at me and Erin, "I think we can safely assume he falls into the non-jerk category."

"Darcy, you kill me." That's as good as a huge thumbs up from my more reserved, measured friend.

"You need to proceed with caution here. Even though he's passed, he could pull a jerk move at any time," Darcy warns, and I half expect a spooky soundtrack to accompany her words.

I stop myself from rolling my eyes. "Yes, I get it. What do you think, Jas?"

Jason sits forward in his seat and leans his arms on the table. "Did anyone else notice he's too focused on food?"

"What?" I say loudly. I readjust my voice to "inside" and "not a child." "What do you mean, too focused on food? That's crazy."

"He mentioned it a lot. Like, too much a lot. I think he might be a feeder."

I'm not sure I want to know the answer, but I ask anyway. "What's a 'feeder?'"

"I thought a feeder was something you put in the garden for the birds," Erin says.

"That's a bird feeder, Erin. An entirely different thing. A feeder is a person, usually a man, who likes to feed his partner up until she gets bigger and bigger and bigger. He's turned on by it."

Darcy arcs an eyebrow. "Really? That's a thing?"

"Look it up." Jason pushes his phone across the table to Darcy. "That guy is a feeder, and he wants Sophie fattened up. I'm sure of it."

I shake my head. What is he talking about? It's ridiculous, that's what it is. "I doubt it, Jas. He's a good guy. Why don't you just admit it?"

"I agree," Erin says firmly. "So what if he likes food? I think it's cute, and Sophie is going to Chez Pierre with him right now. Aren't you, Soph?" Her eyes are bright with excitement for me.

"I am." I stand up. "Thank you for your services this evening, No More Bad Dates Pact Vetting Committee. I'm now going on a date with Oliver Price, the non-jerk, non-feeder," I shoot Jason a look, "and I bet I'm going to have an awesome time." I slip my purse over my shoulder and turn to leave.

"Be sure to eat up," Jason says to my back as I make my way across the floor.

I ignore him. I'm going on a date with a good guy, one of the decent ones. And if my hopes were any higher, I'd have my own atmosphere as I orbited the sun.

Chapter 10

At Chez Pierre a mere ten-minute walk later, I sit at our table for two, gazing at the opulent surrounds. It's just as I imagined: slick, modern, minimal with comfortable fabric chairs tucked under tables covered with crisp white tablecloths. The utensils on the table are so brightly polished I can see myself in them, and the only sound comes from the low murmur of voices and an elderly man playing soft, tasteful piano music on a baby grand in the corner by the bar.

The scene is absolutely primed for romance.

If this goes well, #NoMoreBadDates could be trending for me today in a big, big way.

"This is wonderful," I breathe. "It's like stepping into a slick, modern salon in Paris."

"I'm glad you like it." Oliver smiles across the table at me. "We could speak in French, if you like, to add to the ambiance?"

Speak in French?

Awkwardly, I murmur, "Oh. I, ah, I don't speak French, sorry."

He lets out a light laugh. "That's good, because I don't either." He reaches across the table and takes my hand in his. "I'm glad I passed the test with your friends."

His big hand feels warm wrapped around mine. "Me, too."

"So, I take it you haven't eaten here before?"

I shake my head.

"You're going to love it. The food's amazing." He lets go of my hand and picks the large leather-bound menu up from the table. "How about I order for us? I know what's good here."

I've never been out with a guy who's taken me to a place like this. Swept along by the euphoria of the occasion, I nod and smile dumbly. Oliver immediately waves the waiter over and orders what seems like enough food to keep us from starving for about a month.

"Tell me about yourself, Sophie, and it doesn't have to be how your last relationship ended or anything like that."

I scrunch up my nose. "Sorry about that."

"It's fine. I get it. You need to make sure I'm not a dick."

I laugh. "Well, yes. You can invest so much time in someone only to find they're not who you thought they were."

"Exactly. Now, tell me about your childhood."

"You sound like a shrink."

"No. Just a product marketer," he replies with a glint in his eye.

"Well, I grew up here in Auckland. I'm the youngest of five kids. That means they're always trying to boss me around."

"Five kids? I always wanted a brother. I'm an only child."

"I dreamed of being an only child. All that space and time to myself. Bliss."

"What do you want to know about me?"

We're moving back to him already?

I mentally skim through the list of questions in the No More Bad Dates Pact handbook, but my thoughts keep turning to Jason's "feeder" comment. Which is extremely annoying because it was completely unfounded and really quite ridiculous.

Clearly impatient for my questions, Oliver raises his eyebrows at me. "Well?"

"Okay, I've got one. I'm interested in hearing more about what you like about food."

"What do you mean? Doesn't everyone like food?"

Good point. "Err, well, I mean what about you and food and . . . dating."

Okay, I'm getting weird now. Why did I let Jason get in my head about this guy? First the Danny DeVito comment, which considering Oliver's height is actually quite funny, and now this whole "feeder" business? Whose idea was it to have Jason in on the pact, anyway? Oh, yes, that's right: it was Jason's.

"I'm not sure where you're going with this, Sophie. Are you asking me if I like to go on dates and eat? Because that would be yes, I do." He gestures around the restaurant.

I shoot him a sheepish smile. "Great. That's all I wanted to know. Which I could have worked out for myself, given the fact we're on a date at a restaurant, about to eat some food."

He shoots me a sideways look. "Yeah."

A waiter appears by our table to save me, plates balanced in his hands. "Your appetizers."

With the dishes in front of us—a salmon something or other for me and a beef carpaccio for my date—Oliver waggles his eyebrows and says, "*Bon appétit.* Wow, who knew? I do know how to speak French."

I smile at his weak joke and take a mouthful of my appetizer. It's melt-in-your-mouth delicious. Just as I'm about to take another bite, Oliver loads up his own fork and thrusts it across the table at me. His arms are so long, he doesn't have to reach far, and the forkful hovers a mere inch from my mouth. "Here. Try. Beef carpaccio with capers and celeriac. You'll love it, I promise."

Not knowing what else to do, I open my mouth and take the mouthful. Oliver's right, it is delicious, but I'm on the back foot. Isn't sharing someone else's meal a little too intimate for a first date? I mean, he just fed an almost total stranger from his fork.

Or maybe I'm just a bit on edge. *Damn you, Jason Christie!*

"Amazing, right?" His eyes are wide with expectation.

"Mmm," I say with an enthusiastic nod, my mouth full. I swallow then smile. "Really amazing. Thanks."

I return my attention to my own food and quickly finish it off. It doesn't take long, it is haute cuisine, after all, which is basically code for tiny and outrageously expensive morsels of food.

Pushing Jason from my head, I ask, "So, you used to work with my boss, huh?"

"Paige? Oh yeah, she's the best. I miss her at work. She was always so kind and positive. Never a bad word to say about anyone."

I smile as I think of my sweet, quirky boss who wears her heart on her sleeve and always lives life to the fullest. "That sounds like Paige."

"I've not been to her café, but I bet her food is good. She used to bring baking into the office some days, and it would be gone practically as soon as she opened the tub."

"I bet. She and Bailey specialize in cakes. The Cozy Cottage is known for it."

He takes a bite of his carpaccio then loads up his fork once more—the one he just used to feed himself—and offers me another bite.

"Oh, I'm doing great, thanks."

"You have got to have this. I've added some capers this time. So good."

"I'll, err, take a bite myself." I brandish my fork.

"No no no no no. You don't need to do that. I can feed you. It'll be fun."

Feeling increasingly uncomfortable about him spoon-feeding me, I scoop up a bite on my fork and slip it into my mouth. I chew it and swallow quickly. "No, it's better this way. Thank you for offering. You know, I *am* a grown-up," I add with a laugh. "I've been feeding myself for a while, now." When he doesn't join in the laugh, I add, "It's awkward for you to reach across the table to feed me, anyway." I glance at his Inspector Gadget arms and know it's hardly a stretch for him. Literally.

He pouts. Like a real, kid-style pout. "But it's more fun this way. Don't you think?" His face brightens. "I know what. I've got an idea." He stands, picks up his chair, and moves it so he's sitting next to me. Several people at neighboring tables turn to look at us. I smile feebly at them, feeling powerless to stop this from unfolding.

"See? This way, I don't need to reach across the table." He loads up his fork and hovers it by my lips. "Open up."

I clamp my mouth shut and shake my head like I'm some sort of stubborn toddler refusing her dinner.

"Come on, Sophie. It's good, you know it is."

I shake my head again, with more conviction this time, until Oliver lowers his fork and his head droops. He looks so dejected, I instantly feel bad and want to give him the benefit of the doubt. He passed the Vetting Phase, after all. I'm determined to hold onto this guy.

I place my hand softly on his arm. "It's just a bit too soon for us to do this, that's all. I think sharing a fork is quite intimate. Why don't we get to know each other some more first? Then, one day, I don't know, maybe we could share a milkshake or something?"

His face instantly brightens. "I'd like to share a milkshake with you."

We talk, sitting side by side, and things gradually return to normal. We're two people out on a first date, getting to know one another. No one's feeding anyone else as though they were a baby, and before too long, I forget the initial weirdness and get back to enjoying our date. So much so, by the time our mains are delivered, we're laughing together, and I begin to feel like I could see a future with this guy once more.

"Wow, this pork belly is so good," Oliver comments as he finishes his first mouthful.

"The food here is outstanding. Great choice, Oliver."

"Did you want to try a bite of mine?" Oliver's voice is tentative, and I feel bad that I made such a big deal of it all beforehand. "You can use your own fork, if you prefer?"

"Sure, thanks. You can try my steak, too."

We both sample one another's meals, with our own forks, and agree they're both equally good.

He forks another chunk of my steak from my plate, dips it in the *Sauce Béarnaise*, and before I realize what he's doing, he slips it into my mouth.

He's feeding me *my* food now?

No freaking way.

They say every person has their breaking point. Some can take the heat in the kitchen, some can barely make it through the door into the room. This moment, people, is my breaking point. Who knew a guy who looks like a cross between an oversized Zac Efron and Gerard Butler would deliver it to me?

Before the next forkful makes its way into my mouth, I place my hands against the table, push backwards, and pop up onto my feet.

He blinks up at me, still holding the fork in the air. "Where are you going?"

"I, ah, I just remembered I need to be somewhere. So sorry."

It's a weak excuse. In fact, it barely even qualifies as an excuse, but what else am I going to say? "It's freaking me out the way you keep trying to feed me?" I already tried that approach.

"Can it wait? There's all this to eat." He gestures at the table where our two meals are placed, surrounded by the five side dishes he chose. "And I'm having such a great time with you."

My resolve slips a fraction. "If I'm late to this thing I only just remembered about," I say, persisting with the lie, "will you quit with the feeding?"

He twists his mouth before shaking his head. "I like doing it. It makes me feel close to you. And besides, you're too skinny."

"You're trying to fatten me up?"

He shrugs. "I guess it's my thing."

I nod at him as I let out a resigned puff of air and giant, red flags fly proudly around him. The red flags I refused to see before we got here.

I let out a defeated puff of air. "Of course it is."

Why would a great looking guy with a decent E.Q. and a good job *not* be into weird stuff?

I collect my purse and slip the strap over my shoulder. "Thank you for the date, Oliver. I don't think this is going to work out."

"But what am I meant to do with all this food?"

"Eat it?" I suggest.

The expression on his face is one of complete distaste. "I got it for you."

I glance at the huge amount of food on the table. "I'll pay my half."

He slumps his shoulders in defeat, and I get the distinct feeling this has happened to him before. "Sure. Whatever."

I turn on my heel and walk through the elegant restaurant. With every step, the feeling of unease inside grows and grows. I've been duped by a looney-tunes disguised as one of the good guys.

But what bothers me the most, what really grates me, is that Jason was one hundred percent right.

Chapter 11

On Saturday morning, I arrive at the Cozy Cottage Café bright and early, ready to sink my teeth into my new job. High Tea keeps different hours from its namesake café next door, open Wednesday through Sunday from eleven in the morning—to capture all those people who like to have high tea for lunch—to four in the afternoon. It means I'll be having Mondays and Tuesdays off work and my Saturday night karaoke habit won't be able to run quite as late nor involve quite as much Chardonnay as it once did. Unpleasant experience tells me hangovers and rich treats don't exactly mix.

As the name suggests, the High Tea wing of the Cozy Cottage is focused much more on tea than on coffee. Although we serve both, I know next to nothing about tea, so ever since my bosses offered me the job, I've been researching, sampling, and trying to make myself like it. So far, let's just say it's a work in progress. I'm still a coffee babe, all the way.

"Here, take these." Bailey thrusts a set of keys into my hand. "I'll come through in a moment."

I don't need to know what they unlock.

"Sure," I reply with a burst of happiness. I walk through the café and out onto the street. I stand and gaze at the outside of High

Tea, with its big, gracious windows, its striped awning, and the words "Cozy Cottage High Tea" written in elegant, looping text above the door. I can still barely believe I'll be the one managing this place. Sure, it's only for a couple of days a week, but that's a couple of days a week more than I've ever managed anything in my life.

I close the door behind me and look around the silent room. I take in the quaint wooden tables, the chairs stacked upside down on top. Each table has a potted hyacinth in its center, and scenes of picturesque landscapes are scattered across the walls. It's shabby chic with a country twist, a natural extension of the Cozy Cottage Café next door.

I pick up one of the menus from behind the podium and read through it. It's all about finger food, naturally, with sandwiches and mini scones with jam and cream, an assortment of cakes and slices. All of it delicious, just as I'd expect from any place Paige and Bailey owned.

I walk out into the quaint, covered courtyard. Out here there are white-painted wrought iron tables and chairs, a vertical garden on one wall, and assorted potted plants against the other.

I hear a noise in the main room and make my way back, coming face to face with Paige and her husband, Josh.

"Sophie, good morning!" Paige says.

"Hey, guys. What are you doing here?"

Paige's belly has grown from the last time I saw her. "We've stopped by on our way to meet Marissa and Nash," Paige replies, naming one of the other members of the One Last First Date Pact and her boyfriend.

"And the dog. You can't forget the dog," Josh adds. He shakes his head. "That dog of theirs is treated like some sort of demigod. It eats steak, can you believe?"

"Nash is all about the dogs. He rescues them, you know," Paige explains, although this is information I've known for years. You don't see Nash and Marissa out anywhere without their precious pooch.

She nods at a large plastic tub on one of the tables. "I brought these in. They're little peach tartlets you can serve with chocolate sauce."

"They're good," Josh confirms, "too good."

"I wouldn't know. I couldn't stomach them." Paige scrunches up her nose.

"Morning sickness still giving you grief?" I peer into the tub. The aroma is mouth-watering. "Oh, these look great."

"I'm hoping we'll see the end of it soon. Right, honey?" Paige says.

"Right. We're doing everything we can," he places his hand on Paige's belly, "but these little muffins in here are determined to make sure their presence is known."

Paige puts her hand over Josh's, and they share a loving look. "Did you know I've set Sophie up with a guy I used to work with?" Paige says to her husband.

"I didn't, but it sounds exactly like something my hopeless romantic of a wife would do," he replies with a smile.

She pats him playfully on the arm. "I'm a very good judge of character, and Sophie wants to date nice guys."

"Nice guys, huh?" Josh raises his brows at me, and I nod. "We are a rare breed."

I laugh. "I'm sad to say as a single woman out there in the dating jungle, you are a rare breed, and getting rarer by the minute." I need to bite the bullet, as they say, and come clean with Paige about Oliver. "Actually, I went out with him last night."

Paige's smile is expectant. "And?"

"And it didn't work out." I stave off an involuntary shiver as the memory of him spoon-feeding me returns full force.

"Why not?"

I knew she'd ask, so I have what I hope is a bullet-proof response. "Although you were totally right that he's a great guy, we didn't have any chemistry." No one can argue with that, can they? Chemistry is such an elusive thing.

"No chemistry, huh? Well, you've either got it or you don't. Honey, did you know Sophie's last boyfriend dumped her at Bailey and Ryan's wedding?" she asks Josh. "Can you believe it? I mean, how awful for poor Sophie."

Being labeled "poor Sophie" doesn't exactly make me feel a million dollars, but I smile my way through it.

"At the start or the end of the wedding?" Josh asks me.

"What does that matter?" Paige asks.

"If it's at the end, then maybe he's a better guy for having stuck it out for the night. But then if it's at the start, maybe he was putting her out of her misery early? Actually, now that I think about it, I don't know which is better."

"Neither!" Paige says.

"It was at the start, in the church, around about the time Bailey and Ryan were saying their vows." I smile at them both even though my insides are twisting painfully at the memory.

Josh shakes his head. "What a jerk."

"Oh, it got better. He then went off with another girl, and they spent the reception flirting and dancing in front of everyone, as though she didn't even exist." She tsks. "Flaunting their infatuation, Josh, right in front of poor Sophie."

Again with the "poor Sophie." I could get a complex here.

I shoot them both a smile that I hope says "I'm totally over it, now let's move on." I collect the tub in my hands. "Thanks for these. I need to get things started in here. High Tea waits for no man. Well, no woman. Most of our customers are female."

"I know you're going to do an amazing job," Paige says to me. "I couldn't trust our High Tea baby with anyone else." To my surprise, Paige's eyes begin to fill with tears. "It means a lot to me that you're doing this, Sophie."

I look from Paige to Josh.

"Paige is feeling a little emotional right now." Josh wraps his arm around Paige's shoulders. "Shall we go meet the others? See what lavish meal that dog of theirs ate for breakfast?"

She nods and they turn to leave. She glances back at me and mouths, "Thank you." I wave them off with a smile.

By opening time, waitress Matilda has arrived, and our chef, Clive, is in the kitchen with Bailey, baking things that smell like they could add five inches to my thighs—and sadly, they probably will. I'm dashing around ensuring all the little details are right: the gold fringe on the menus are hanging downwards, there are no dead flowers or leaves on the vertical wall, and the silverware is clean and orderly on each table. Me? O.C.D.? Well, maybe a little.

"Are you ready for this?" Bailey asks as I tie my High Tea apron around my waist in the kitchen. "Our first customers will be here in a few minutes."

"I think I am. I mean, I've worked in here before, but it feels different now, you know?"

"You weren't a manager then."

I do my best to ignore the pang of nerves inside. "Right."

Bailey calls a mini staff meeting. "Today is a dry run for Sophie, who will take over fully tomorrow if she's confident to do so. If you need anything, go to her first. I'll be out here doing the prep with Clive. Okay with you, Sophie?"

I guess it'll have to be.

I nod and plaster on a confident smile. "Sure. No problem."

"Right, well, good luck, and enjoy yourselves," Bailey says with her characteristic beautiful smile.

I take my place at the podium, ready to welcome our first customers of the day. When some familiar faces push through the door, I rush to greet them. "You guys! What are you doing here?" I greet Darcy, Erin, and Jason with quick hugs.

Erin beams at me. "We wanted to be here to support you on your first big day."

"That and we knew you had that totally sucky date with the weirdo guy last night," Darcy adds.

I roll my eyes. "Don't remind me."

"We're your first customers," Jason announces with evident pride.

"But there's only one table for three booked right now, and that's for . . . oh, I get it. You're Ms. Agnetha."

"That's right," Erin says. "May I introduce Frida," she points at Erin who strikes a classic ABBA pose, "And Jason's Bjorn."

"Being fake members of ABBA sounded like it'd be a lot more

fun," he says. "I was expecting private jets, a stadium full of adoring fans, maybe a bucket load of cash."

"Hey, don't complain, Jas. At least we didn't make you wear the seventies flares," Darcy says.

Jason laughs. "That's a very good point. Praise the Lord for small mercies."

I collect the menus in my arms. "Shall I show you to your table, Agnetha, Frida, and Bjorn?"

Darcy flashes me her grin. "Thank you very much, Ms. McCarthy. You're the manager here, I understand."

I beam back at her. "Why, yes, I am." I show them to their table.

As they take their seats, Jason says, "I have a feeling we're going to tip super well today. Don't you, ladies?"

I blush and smile. "You guys!"

"This place is just like the café next door," Jason comments as he looks around.

"Funny that, Einstein," Darcy replies. "For a doctor, you sure can be slow on the uptake."

"Thanks a lot!" he protests.

"Slow but super pretty," I tease.

Jason's eyes flash to mine. "I'm glad you think so, McCarthy. I aim to please."

I shake my head at him good-naturedly. "Okay, Matilda, your server, will be over in a moment." I turn to leave, stop, and turn back. "You guys are the best, you know that? Thanks for being here."

"Sophie McCarthy's big moment? We wouldn't miss it," Erin says.

"Exactly," Darcy agrees.

Jason nods and smiles up at me, saying, "We've got your back, McCarthy."

We're kept steady into the early afternoon, but I notice there are more than a couple of empty tables at any given time. With Bailey and Paige's delicious cooking and reputation as the queens of cake, I'd expected it to be busier. During a lull, I manage to grab a few minutes to check in on my friends.

"I still can't believe he was a 'feeder,'" Erin says as she places her teacup back on its saucer. "I didn't even know what that was. And now, I wish I didn't, for your sake, Soph. I mean, *ugh*."

I shake my head. "It just goes to show you can vet someone and question them and think they're sane human beings, and they can still have some weird thing, lurking deep down inside." I look at Jason, fully expecting an "I told you so." Which is precisely what I get.

"I told you so, McCarthy," he says. "Would you listen to your much more mature, expert guest judge? That would be a 'no.'"

"Not helping, Jason." I let out a heavy sigh. "Last night was almost enough to make you want to give up."

"Give up?" Darcy says. "On dating?"

"Yes. No. Oh, I don't know."

"Sit," Darcy instructs. "We need to talk this out." She turns to Jason. "And no more from you, thank you."

"Got it," he says with a serious nod.

I glance around the room and check that Bailey doesn't need me. She's chatting to a customer herself, and the people at the tables around us have all been served and are currently tucking into their High Tea treats. I've got a few minutes, so I pull out a chair and sit down with my friends. "Okay, convince me I'm being dramatic."

"It was one date gone wrong. That's all. We missed what should have been a red flag," Darcy says.

"Jason didn't miss it. He called it, and I didn't listen to him," I reply.

All eyes at the table turn to Jason. He simply shrugs, his mouth firmly shut.

"It's good to see you can do what you're told," Darcy says to him. "We didn't believe him because it seemed so crazy."

My mind turns to the way Oliver kept thrusting food at my face, and I shiver. "It *is* crazy."

Darcy shakes her head. "That's no reason to give up, babe. We just need to tighten the Vetting Process."

"Exactly," Erin says with confidence. "You need to get back on that horse, stat! You're our guiding star in this right now. And all that's happened is that a slippery one got through the net, that's all. A little, slippery, slithery fish."

"A weird little, slippery, slithery fish," I correct.

"I think you need to go out and find someone straight away. And I bet when you do, this one will be a keeper," Erin says.

"I don't want a keeper. Well, a short-term-keeper, I guess, not a husband-keeper."

"Of course," Erin says as she sits back in her seat. "That's what I meant." She casts her eyes down, and I begin to wonder whether she actually wants her H.E.A. and not just an H.F.N.

I'm too wrapped up in my own date-related sulk to question her on it.

"Do you want my opinion?" Jason asks.

I shrug. "Sure. Why not?" He's managed to stay quiet for some time, so it's the least I can do.

"Give it some time. If you go out looking for the right guy, chances are you won't find him."

"He's wrong," Erin states simply. "Find that horse and climb up on him."

"Now, there's an image," I reply with a grin.

The door opens and a group of people are almost blown into the room along with some leaves from the trees outside. It's that time of the year. It's cooling off, the leaves are falling, and it'll only be a matter of time before we get the fire blazing in the café, making it even more cozy.

I stand up. "I'd better get back to work."

"You go do your thing, babe. Karaoke at eight tonight," Darcy says.

"Who knows? You might meet your next date there," Erin says with a waggle of her eyebrows.

Darcy looks up at me. "You've got to promise not to be defeated after just one date, okay? Like Erin said, you've got to get back on that horse."

"Horse. Right. See you tonight at eight." I tighten my pink Cozy Cottage High Tea apron around my waist as I make my way through the tables to the podium. There's a group of people waiting when I get there. "Welcome to Cozy Cottage High Tea. How may I help you today?"

"We've got a booking for five people under the name Samson," one of the two younger women says.

I peer at the computer screen and spot the booking. I look up and smile at the older woman in the group. "Happy birthday, Mrs. Samson. We're so pleased you chose to spend your afternoon with us here at High Tea."

"Oh, thank you, dear," Mrs. Samson replies with a big smile. "My family is treating me."

"You deserve it, dear," says the older man at her side.

"Mom's wanted to come here forever," her son says to me. "Every time we drive by it's always 'doesn't that place look nice,' and 'I wonder what high tea is like.'"

"It's true. Subtle is not a word we use with you a whole lot, Mom," one of the daughters says.

I smile at them all, the sweet, happy family here to make their mother's birthday special. "Well, subtle or not, we're glad you're here, Mrs. Samson. Please, follow me."

I collect five menus from behind the desk and lead them to a table by the window I had reserved for them. When her son made the booking, he had told me it was her birthday, and we've prepared a special High Tea cake for her at his request.

"Thanks for this," the son says to me as the rest of his family take their seats. He extends his hand and we shake. "I'm David, by the way. We spoke on the phone. It's great to put a face to the voice." He keeps a hold of my hand for a second longer and adds, "A real pretty one."

My eyes dart to his face, and I notice his smile is a little flirty. He's cute in a Nick Jonas kind of way, only a little taller than me, with the bluest eyes I've ever seen outside of an American Girl doll.

"Thank you," I say, not quite sure how else to react. I'm still smarting from the whole Oliver feeder debacle.

He chuckles when he says, "You're welcome?"

I find my cheeks heating up. What was it that Erin said? Get back on that horse?

"I-I hope you enjoy your high tea experience."

"I'm sure we will." He takes his seat at the table, and I get back to my work.

Sometime later, when I steal a look at him from across the room, he smiles at me, and I get a couple of butterflies batting their wings inside.

Butterflies? Really?

Wow, even I'm impressed with how quickly I've moved on.

After a virtual fully blown conversation through simply glancing at smiling at one another over the next hour and a half, it comes as no surprise when David hangs back after paying the check while his family assembles outside.

"I hope your mom had an enjoyable afternoon."

"She did. I did, too, although for other reasons, I bet." His smile is just as flirty as it was when he arrived, and I happily return it. Sue me: flirting is fun, and I've picked my horse.

I feign innocence. "What would those reasons be?"

"Give me your number and I'll tell you."

Well, that's direct and to the point. I don't need to be asked twice—did I mention how cute this guy is?—so I recite my number as he types it into his phone.

"Got it." He slips his phone into his back pocket. "Hey, do you like the beach? Swimming? That sort of thing?"

"Who doesn't?" Although I need to spend some serious time getting to know a guy before I'll parade around in front of him in anything less than full clothing, thank you very much.

He grins at me. "Awesome. I'll text you. See you soon, Sophie."

I raise my hand in a small wave and say a goodbye as I watch him leave. My hopes that David might turn out to be a good guy rise inside me like an over-heated hot air balloon.

Chapter 12

After the last customer has gone home, full to the brim of our treats, we clean the place up so it's spotless. Matilda and Clive have just left for the day, and I find Bailey sitting at one of the tables and staring at her laptop. She looks like she's concentrating hard.

"All done," I say.

She looks up at me and smiles. "Sophie. How do you feel today went?"

"So good!" I reply in total honesty. From my besties turning up to support me, to meeting cute and flirty David, to the last customers' gushing compliments about the mini cupcakes, it was an awesome day. "Everything went really, really well. I had a great day."

"That's great to hear! You can't expect it to run like that every time, of course, but I'm so glad it went well for you today."

"Me too."

She nods, her mouth drawn into a line as she returns her attention to her laptop screen. "Right now, I need to get on with some work. Are you any good with numbers?"

I walk around the table to look at the screen. It's a spreadsheet, full columns of numbers. "That looks complicated."

"Oh, it is. So complicated." She lets out a sigh. "It's all part of managing two businesses, I guess. This is something Josh set up for the Cozy Cottage, and I'm trying to apply it to High Tea. This column here shows what we're spending to feed and water all those customers of ours, this shows what we're making, and these here show things like staff and non-food-related running costs."

I run my eyes over the numbers. I did some accounting as part of my finance degree, so it all makes sense to me. I'm surprised to see the profits are not as high as I would have expected for such a successful business.

"Let's be honest," Bailey says as she watches me study the screen, "profits are down a little these days. We started out with a flurry, and it felt like we could do no wrong, but over the last six to nine months, well, the café has been carrying High Tea."

"Why do you think that is?"

She lets out a sigh. "I do not know. Paige and I have wracked our brains. She knows how to market, our website is great, we do special deals to bring more customers in. A whole lot of things. Plus, the café has never been so busy. But here? Something's just not working. Not the way it used to, anyway."

"I thought going out to high tea was the new thing in Auckland. It's super fashionable."

"Maybe that's the problem? When we opened, this was the only place doing high tea in this part of town. Now, I could name three places within a short drive."

"But it's so special here! It's got your amazing food, which you are totally famous for, plus it's so cute and homey."

Bailey shakes her head. "I don't know. As owners, it's up to Paige and me to work it out, but if you have any ideas…"

"That sounds like a challenge to me. I'd be more than happy to put some thought into it. I could come up with some ideas?"

Yup, I'm either super positive or super eager. I'm not sure which right now.

Bailey laughs. "I love your attitude, Sophie. I'll let you know." She snaps her laptop shut. "Shall we get out of here? I have a new husband waiting for me at home, and he's promised to take me to a movie at the Italian Film Festival tonight. My choice, so it'll be a romantic one."

"You are so lucky. You have no idea."

She stands up. "Believe me, this is only the second time in our entire relationship he's agreed to go to a romantic movie with me. I really had to twist his arm." She tucks her laptop under her arm. "Have a great night, Sophie. You deserve it."

With Bailey gone, I'm left on my own once more. I look around me, ideas on how to make this place pop rolling through my mind.

If it's a challenge, I'm up for it. I love this place as if it were my own, and I want it to survive. No, forget that. I *need* it to survive. And I'm going to do whatever I can to make sure that happens.

⸻

"WHO ARE YOU TEXTING? Your phone is going crazy right now."

I glance at Jason as I slip my phone behind one of the scatter cushions on the sofa. "No one."

We're at our apartment, relaxing on the sofa. After my big day at High Tea, I'm too shattered to go to karaoke with my girls. Instead, I chose a quiet night in, playing video games with Jason.

"Well, 'no one' needs to stop with the endless messages because we've got a game to play here." He hands me the game controller as my phone vibrates against the cushion. "*Seriously*, McCarthy."

Despite Jason's protestations—and maybe because of them, too —I pull my phone out once more and read the most recent message.

You're cute, you know that?

I smile as my cheeks flush warm. I type out a quick reply.

No, you are.

Ever since we met this afternoon, David and I have been texting up a flirtatious storm of monsoon proportions. The whole "play it cool" thing is clearly not his style. We've covered all the main topics: favorite drink, music preferences, and whether the Kardashians are sucking the lifeblood from the planet with their narcissism and inexplicable appeal (verdict: a very clear and unanimous yes).

And what's more, he's nice. Really, really nice.

I have extremely high hopes, people. *Extremely* high hopes.

"Okay, hand it over." Jason holds his hand out, palm-up in front of me.

"What? No." I place my phone back behind the cushion once more. "It's battle time. Prepare to have your cute little hiney whooped, Christie."

"That's fighting talk."

I shrug. "You know I'm good for it."

My phone vibrates once more, and I go to collect it from its hiding place. I hesitate, my hand mid-air, and glance at Jason. "Pause the game, please."

"Oh, no you don't." Before I know what's happening, he throws himself across me, pulls my phone from behind the cushion, and jumps up, brandishing it in the air.

"Hey! Give it back!" I stand up and reach for my phone, but Jason has a good few inches on me, so I only manage to bat at his elbow. It achieves absolutely nothing.

"You can have it back once we've played," he says as I jump up to try to grab it from him.

"But this is important." And yes, my voice does sound like a whine.

"Important, huh?" He reads the screen. "'You've got beautiful hair.'" He shoots me a questioning look. "This is what's important? And who the heck is this David Crichton guy, anyway?" He waggles the phone at me.

"I told you. He's no one."

"That's not going to cut it with me, McCarthy. You've been sitting there on the sofa, giggling and blushing for far too long for him to be no one. How do I know he's not some weirdo with a hair fetish who's planning on shaving your head to harvest your hair while you sleep?"

I laugh. "Because that would be insane?"

"You've dated worse, the least of all being that feeder guy."

"Please, don't remind me."

"So, who is Davy Crocket?"

"His name is not Davy Crockett, it's David Crichton."

"Same thing. You should check to see if he's the King of the Wild Frontier and wears a furry hat."

An image of David with a hat made from raccoon fur pops into my head. "Thank you for that, Jason." My tone drips with sarcasm.

"As your older, wiser, and significantly more mature roommate, I need to know what his intentions are toward you."

I extend my hand. "Pass me my phone, and I'll tell you all about him."

He passes me my phone, and I keep up my end of the bargain. "I met him today at High Tea. He spent the whole time smiling across the room at me, and then he asked for my number. Isn't that adorable?"

"Adorable," he deadpans.

I ignore him. "David is the horse Erin told me to get back up on."

"You're clearly not taking my advice to have a break from looking for this whole H.F.G.L.T. thing."

"It's H.F.N., Jas, and no, I'm not. We're going on a date."

"You mean an Initial Meeting. As part of the No More Bad Dates Pact Committee, you need to stick with the rules, Ms. McCarthy."

I wave my hand in the air. "I guess. But maybe I don't need to do the whole pact thing with him? I can tell he's a good one."

"Like you could with the feeder?"

"Well, no." Why does he have to be right? "But this is different," I sniff.

"Really? Was it like you could tell with Andrew dump-me-at-a-wedding Foster?"

He's on a roll now, dredging up my most recent dating failures.

Jason Christie is not good for my ego, that's for sure.

I let out a puff of air and my mouth twists. Even though I'm annoyed at him right now, I know he's got a point. Damn him! My track record of judging whether a guy is a weirdo, a jerk, or just plain horrible is poor at best. "Yeah, okay. I'll make it an Initial Meeting."

"Do you pinky promise?" He waggles his little finger at me as though we're a couple of school kids.

"I thought you said you're the mature one?"

"I am. Now pinky promise."

I laugh as I hook my smallest finger around his. It's strange, but our fingers hooked together feels somehow right, like they fit. See? I said it's strange.

"I pinky promise. I'll have an Initial Contact with David and let him know about the Vetting Process."

"Good. Not that it worked last time. If only Darcy and Erin had listened to their knowledgeable and wise friend, Jason. Or should I start calling myself the Dating Oracle? Oh, yeah. I like the sound of that: Dating Oracle, Doctor Jason Christie."

I roll my eyes. "Don't let it go to your head, dude."

"Too late." He flashes me that cheeky grin of his. "So, this Davy Crocket guy. What's so different about him?"

I feel my cheeks begin to heat. "I guess he seems so nice. He and his sisters took their mom to High Tea for her birthday today. He arranged the whole thing. That's pretty sweet of him, don't you think?"

"So, the guy loves his mom? Stop the press; this is huge!"

"Us women like it when guys love their moms. It means they've got serious dating potential."

"Well, us guys know he's probably just a big old mommy's boy."

I whack him playfully on the arm. "He's not a mommy's boy. He's sweet and smart, and funny and flirty."

"Well, of course he's going to be flirty with you. You're a total babe."

I widen my eyes. "I am?"

"You know you are. But I'm not going to make your head so big you can't fit through the kitchen door to grab me another Coke."

I laugh. "Did you seriously just flatter me so I would go to the kitchen for you?"

He pulls his best Puss-in-Boots wide-eyed look. "Did it work?"

I waggle one of the controllers in my hand. "How about the loser of the game has to get the Cokes?"

"Well, in that case, you may as well go get that drink for me now because you are going *down*, McCarthy."

"Fighting talk, princess. Now, let's get on with your humiliation."

"Brave words from the reigning loser."

"I prefer to be called 'second place holder,' thank you very much."

Sitting side by side, we start the game up and not even my phone vibrating with another message from David can distract me from my attempt to beat Jason. I'm totally focused, shooting, smashing, destroying. Jason's the reigning apartment *Fortnite* champion, as he loves to remind me, and I've been working all year to dislodge him from his number one spot. I've managed it twice, and seeing him sulk those two times made it all completely worthwhile.

But, sadly, today is not my day, and I sit waiting for him to laud his win over me, which he does at his patronizing best.

"Oh, McCarthy. What's the saying? Always the loser, never the champ?"

I shake my head in good humor at him. Although I would love to beat him at this game, it doesn't bother me enough to lose any sleep over it. "Yeah, something like that, Jas." I push myself up off the sofa. "I'll get your Coke, and then I'm heading to bed. I am beat."

With a yawn, I wander into the kitchen to get him his drink. I hand it to him and say, "Good night."

"I'm looking forward to vetting Davy Crockett," he calls down the hall.

"Not Davy Crockett," I call back as I close my bedroom door behind me.

I flop down on my bed next to a sleeping Freckles. She looks up at me briefly before snuggling back into a furry ball. I lie on my bed, pull out my phone, and read the last message from David. Anticipation spreads through me like warm lava.

I think I've found one of the good guys, and nothing Jason or anyone else can say will persuade me otherwise.

Chapter 13

The No More Bad Dates Pact Rules of Engagement state clearly that Initial Contact needs to take place over coffee, preferably at a coffee house. Today, with David, I've bent the rules a teensy little bit. Sure, we're sitting together, talking over piping hot cups of coffee. So far, so per the rulebook. But instead of meeting at a café, we're sitting on the beautiful golden-sand beach of Mission Bay, a well-heeled beach not far from the central city.

With our takeout coffees in hand, waves rhythmically crashing against the shore, the scent in the air is salty and fresh, and I'm finding it hard to tear my eyes from David's handsome face as he tells me about his life.

"So, although I'm no longer working directly with sea life in my new management job, I'm still really involved and get to spend time by the tanks most days."

"This is at the aquarium?"

"Yup. Right over there." He nods in the direction of the city.

I can't keep the admiration from my voice when I say, "It must be so great to have a career where you're doing what you love."

"Oh, it is. If you love what you do, you won't work a day in your life, as the saying goes. Don't you love managing the high tea place?

You seemed really happy there on Saturday. But maybe that was just because of the guy who kept smiling at you?"

The hopeful look on his face has a giggle bubbling up inside me. "Oh, I'm sure it's all down to you. But in addition to the fact I got to meet you there, I do love it at High Tea. I worked next door at the Cozy Cottage Café for years, too. But it's not a 'career.'" I use air quotes as I let out a sigh. "At least, not if you're my family. They want me to do something more important with my life than serving food and drinks to people."

"What could be more important than loading people up with tea, sugar, and carbs, and sending them home happy?"

My grin is so broad, it threatens to crack my face in two. "My point exactly."

We sit, smiling at one another, as thoughts like "he gets me!" and "this could totally work!" dart around my head like a couple of ping pong balls.

Yup, I like this guy. Like, *really* like him. He's funny and cute and smart, and what's more, he's got humility, which is something I think I've seen in a guy my age maybe once in my life. I apologize to the males of my generation, but it's the truth, sad as it is.

He looks out at the sea. "I love the beach. Everything about it. It's where I feel the most 'me.'" David's cheeks flush an attractive shade of pink, making his blue eyes stand out even more in the bright sun. "Sorry if that sounds a bit too sappy."

"Oh, it's not sappy at all. It's what I'd expect of a marine biologist. I think it's amazing." The wind whips my hair around my face. I shove it behind my ears and grin at him. "I really like the beach, too."

"I'm so happy to hear that, Sophie." David beams at me as though I've paid him the highest compliment possible, not just told him that, along with billions of other people, I like the beach.

"You know, you should grow your hair longer. It's so pretty. You'd look incredible with long, flowing hair. Like Daryl Hannah in *Splash*. You know, the eighties mermaid movie?"

Not sure how to take it, I mutter, "Err, thanks."

If he notices my hesitation, he doesn't show it.

"Do you swim or surf?" I ask. With his broad shoulders and slim physique, he's definitely got a swimmer's vibe going on.

"I like to get in amongst it, you know? Feel at one. Get in touch with the essence of the ocean."

I pretend I know what he's talking about. "Right. Yes. The essence of the ocean. Totally."

Isn't that salt?

"So, swimming then?" I continue, still not exactly sure what he's going on about.

"Yup. Swimming. But I scuba dive, too."

"You're a regular Jacques Cousteau."

"I wish! He's my hero."

"I bet he is." I drain the last of my coffee and glance at my watch. Even though I could happily sit here all day with David, I need to get to the Cozy Cottage for a shift. Short-staffed, Bailey called me in desperation last night, and I was more than happy to help out.

"This has been really great. Thanks for meeting up with me. Maybe next time you'll let me make you dinner?" he asks.

"You cook, too? Is there nothing you can't do?" Suddenly nervous, I add, "About next time. I, ah, need to ask you something."

"This sounds serious. Are you going to reveal some fascinating hidden truth to me?"

I let out a jittery laugh. "Oh, nothing like that. It's no big deal really."

David's eyes are dancing when he replies, "Pity. I like a woman of mystery."

"Sorry to disappoint. You see, I've got a crummy track record with dating, and, well, here's the thing." I know I need to just come out and say it, so I force myself to go on. "I need you to meet my friends first before I can go on a date with you." I hold my breath and look for his reaction out of the corner of my eye.

"You need me to meet your friends before we can go on a second date?"

"Yes. That's right." I'm not about to go into the whole Initial Contact versus First Date thing with him. Totally unnecessary right now. "They'll ask you a few questions, nothing too tricky. I'll be there, too. Is that okay?"

I know I sound like a crazy person, asking a guy I've had one coffee and a bunch of flirty texts with to meet my friends, but I promised Jason—an unbreakable pinky promise at that, the most serious of all promises, as we all know—and I need to be committed to the Pact.

He studies my face for a moment before he replies, "I'm not sure why exactly, but if it's what you want, I can meet your friends."

Relief floods through me. "Thank you!" I lurch myself toward him until I remember the No More Bad Dates Pact rule decreeing that there should be no physical contact during Initial Contact. I pull back and shoot him a sheepish grin. I must look like I'm doing some sort of weird dance move. "That's, ah, great."

David shoots me a questioning look. "You okay, Sophie?"

"Oh, yes. Absolutely." In embarrassment, I push myself up and brush sand from my butt. "I'll set something up with my friends and let you know, okay?"

He stands up beside me. "Sure. Then, once I pass with flying colors, I'm going to cook you my signature dish."

"You have a signature dish?" I don't have enough dishes in my repertoire to have a "signature dish." Heck, outside of my limited toast repertoire, I don't have any "dishes" whatsoever.

"I do salmon steaks done in marmalade with brown sugar. They are so good."

As we make our way back to the sidewalk, my mouth begins to water. "I figured as a marine biologist, you'd be against eating fish. I mean, you love them so much, right?"

"There's an order to everything. We humans are at the apex of the food chain, much as a whale is in the oceans, or a lion on the plains of Africa."

Forget Jacques Cousteau, this guy is a regular David Attenborough.

"This was fun. Let me know what works for you, and I'll be there ready to answer any question your friends throw at me."

Relief washes over me like the surf on the shore. "You're awesome, you know that?"

He gives a shrug and shoots me one of his knee-weakening smiles. "I try."

As I say goodbye to him and return to my car, the happiness he's sparked in me subsides as my insides begin to knot with tension. The way Oliver passed the test and still turned out to be a looney-tunes plays on my mind. We'll need to be extra vigilant with David, because I have high hopes for this guy, and more than anything, I want him to pass.

Chapter 14

"Two Initial Contacts versus zero for me and Erin. You're on a roll, girl!" Darcy high fives me from her barstool across the table at O'Reilly's Pub, and I beam back at her.

"Problem is, this one may turn out to be a total weirdo, too. Right, McCarthy?" Jason drapes an arm around my shoulders and gives me a quick squeeze.

"No, he won't!" I protest as Erin tells him not to be so cynical and Darcy tells him not to be such an ass. (Darcy is always more direct when it comes to insults. It's something I've long admired about her.)

"Tell us more about this guy, Sophie," Erin says.

"His name is Davy Crockett, he wears a hat made out of a dead animal, and he's the King of the Wild Frontier," Jason says before I have the chance to reply.

"I told you; stop being an ass," Darcy repeats.

I pat him patronizingly on his arm. "Be a good boy and get the drinks in, Christie."

"I know when I'm not needed." He shrugs and moves to the bar to place our order.

"Okay, with Mr. Cynical gone, tell us everything," Erin says. "Is he cute? I bet he's cute."

Warmth spreads through my belly as I think of David on the beach, his hair moving in the breeze, his face flushed as he talked about what he loved. "He is cute, really cute, and he's super smart and successful. He's a marine biologist and runs a team at the aquarium. He's so passionate about what he does. It's really hot."

"A regular Aquaman, huh? Don't tell me he looks like Jason Momoa. If he does, I might just die right here at O'Reilly's." Darcy has a major thing for Jason Momoa. If David did look like him, I'm sure Darcy would already have tracked him down.

"No to Momoa," I reply with a shake of my head. "But you'll see for yourself when he's here, which will be really soon." My nerves kick up a notch.

"You like this one," Erin teases.

Darcy examines my face. "Yeah, she does."

"She liked the last one too, and look at how that worked out." Jason places the drinks in front of us. He lowers his voice and says with an accent, "Come with me and I'll feed you until you're the size of a house."

I laugh. "What's with the accent? Are you trying to be *Terminator* Arnold Schwarzenegger?"

Jason grins. "I was trying to sound like a psycho, but I'll take Arnie."

I roll my eyes. "For the millionth time, Jas, he wasn't a feeder. He just wanted to feed me my meal, like I was a baby." I shift in my seat. "And yes, I heard it. That's not a whole lot better."

"Poor Soph," Erin says. "This next guy is going to be one of the good ones."

Jason takes a swig from his bottle of beer. "What do we know about him?"

I look over at the entrance to the bar and spot David at the door. He's scanning the room, looking just as cute as he did that day on the beach, and I feel my anticipation rise. "We know he's here." I stand up and wave.

When he spots me, his face breaks into a grin, and he strides confidently over to the table. He greets me with a chaste kiss to the cheek, and I feel every set of my friends' eyes on me. "Hi, Sophie. You're looking gorgeous tonight."

"Oh, this old thing?" I reply, pulling out the lamest—and most dishonest—line known to female kind as I paw at the brand-new blouse I bought yesterday.

"She does look gorgeous, you're totally right," Erin coos. "Hi, David. I'm Erin, this is Jason, and this is Darcy."

As I take a nervous chug of my Chardonnay for courage, David smiles and says hello to everyone before taking his seat at the table.

"So, this is new; meeting the friends before the second date."

I will Darcy not to pick him up on it. She's not listening to the "don't tell him it was an Initial Contact" message I'm shooting her repeatedly via telepathy. She places her palms on the table on either side of her glass of Pinot Noir. As her friend of many years, it's a gesture I'm all too familiar with. It's her "let me explain" gesture. Which is exactly what she does. "David. You had what we call an Initial Contact with Sophie. A short meeting for compatibility research purposes. It clearly went well enough for you to be here now. If you pass this Vetting Process, then you'll get to go on your First Date with her. Make sense?"

Have I mentioned that Darcy can sometimes have a carrot up her butt? Because, OMG, Darcy can sometimes have *such* a carrot up her butt.

Seemingly unfazed, David replies, "That's good to know. I'd always wondered what a coffee with a potential date should be called. Now that I know, I'll never call it anything but Initial Contact." His eyes sparkle as they flash to mine.

I press my lips together to stop a giggle from escaping. I love Darcy, she's one of my besties and I would do anything for her, but she can be more than a little uptight about things. Sometimes I wish she'd just go with the flow more, like Erin and me.

"I've got a question," Jason begins and I close my eyes and say a silent prayer that he's not going to be difficult. "Are you someone who likes to feed women their dinner?"

"Feed women their dinner?" he guffaws.

"You know, scoop it up in a spoon and literally feed it to her.

Kinda like she's a baby," Jason explains.

"No," David says with a laugh, and I beam at him. "That's just weird."

Jason taps his chin as though deep in thought. "We're glad to hear that, David."

"Okay, now we've got *that* cleared up, shall we begin in earnest?" Darcy asks.

David leans back on his stool. "Do your worst."

As much as I like David, I don't want to be here for his interrogation. Part of me wants to stay to protect him from the coming onslaught, and part of me—the part that wins—wants to be far, far away. "I'll go get you a drink. What would you like?"

"I'll take a beer, thanks. Same as Jason's."

"Flattery will get you everywhere," Jason says with a smirk. "Does that mean I get to ask the first *earnest* question?"

David replies with, "Sure," as I make my way over to the bar.

I wait at the busy bar for a long time as the two barmen make what appear to be ever-increasingly complicated drinks for a group of girls out on a hen's night. They're laughing and joking among themselves, the bride-to-be dressed in a plastic tiara and veil. Eventually, after not one but two of the merry hens accidentally step on my sandal-clad feet, I place my order.

Back at the table, I put the beer in front of David as he's regaling my friends with a story about a school of sharks he "met" while diving in Sydney Harbor. Although it sounds like my own personal kind of hell to be deep down in the dark water, surrounded by sharks, my friends are riveted. As I sit down on my stool, I allow myself a small smile at what that might mean for David and me.

"Where else have you dived?" Erin asks.

"I started out on the Great Barrier when I was a teenager. It was an amazing experience, and I'm so lucky to have had the opportunity to get my ticket there. If you haven't visited the Great Barrier, you should go, like, immediately. It will blow your mind."

"Where else?" Jason asks.

"Cozumel, Mexico. That's stunning."

"Oh, I'd love to go to Mexico," I say.

"Do you dive?" David asks me.

"Ah, no. The idea of being deep under the water like that with just a tube to breathe through isn't my idea of fun. I snorkel, though." Well, I've snorkeled once, and I got freaked out when some seaweed skimmed my legs. But David doesn't need to know that.

His face lights up as a chuckle escapes from his lips. "It's a start. I can work with that."

We share a moment in which we gaze into one another's eyes, and I imagine myself all sleek and tan post dive on the back of a boat off the coast of somewhere exotic with him, discussing all the fish we've seen in the watery depths.

"Remember when Sophie got a totally sunburnt butt when we went snorkeling in Rarotonga a couple of years back?" Darcy asks unhelpfully. "Remember, Soph? You couldn't sit down for days without some serious wincing."

I shift in my seat at the memory of that bright red, raw, stinging burn. "Thanks for reminding me."

"Is that why you walked around the apartment like a bear with a sore head when you got back from that trip?" Jason asks.

"More like a bear with a sore butt," Darcy says with a laugh.

I glance at David's amused face before I say, "Yes, thank you, *friends*. Not helping. And anyway, aren't you meant to be asking David questions? Not humiliating *me*?"

"Sorry, Soph," Darcy says. "But you've got to admit, it was funny."

I shoot her a look. "Not so funny for me."

"So, David, getting back to what we were talking about before," Erin leads, "before we got onto the diving stories."

"Ah, yes. The whole 'am I a decent enough guy to date Sophie' thing." David flashes me a smile, and my cheeks heat up.

"That's the one," Erin replies. "Would you say you're honest with women you date?"

"Totally. With me, what you see is what you get. If you're not going to be honest, what's the point?"

"Exactly!" Darcy's enthusiasm is obvious. "You see? This is what we're looking for, right, girls?"

Erin and I nod.

"Why don't more guys have that attitude?" Darcy directs this question at Jason and David.

"Um, because all men are horrible human beings who aren't even worth the leftovers on your plates?" Jason offers.

Darcy waves his comment away with her hand. "Total hyperbole."

"I can't tell you, but I'm not sure you're right, Jason. All I know is honesty is really important to me," David replies.

I beam at him. So far, so incredibly good. "Awesome."

"Okay, so considering you're honest, tell us, are you into anything weird?" Erin asks.

David knits his brows together. "Weird?"

"You know, hobbies, activities, things that other people might not be so open to?" Erin clarifies.

He lifts one side of his mouth as he looks around the table at us. I hold my breath. He's clearly considering whether to share something right now, and I'm hoping against all hope it's not going to be a deal breaker.

"David?" I question.

"Full disclosure, right? Otherwise there's no point in moving forward with this thing," he says.

Please don't be a weirdo, please don't be a weirdo, please don't be a weirdo.

Jason leans back and crosses his arms. "This is gonna be interesting."

"I hope it'll be illuminating for you all, actually. A different way to look at the world, maybe?" David says.

My smile is weak and forced. "What are you talking about, David?"

"Like you, Sophie, I'm looking for someone special, someone who can share my passions," he begins.

"Like diving?" I ask, hopeful. Diving might not be my favorite thing, but at least it's not weird.

"More than diving," David explains. "It's a lifestyle, really. Something I committed to a couple of years back. In fact, I celebrated my two-year anniversary of living this way only last month.

It was a super special day." He turns to me. "If you're who I think you are, who I *hope* you are, I believe you could have shared that moment with me in a really beautiful way, Sophie."

My hopes drop to my shoes. *Uh-oh. Alert! Alert!*

Jason leans his elbows on the table. "Okay, dude. Enough preamble. Give it to us straight."

David's face is bright when he states simply, "I live my life as much as I can in the world of merfolk."

Merfolk?

Oh, no no no no no no.

There's a stunned silence around the table as our jaws collectively drop.

"In the world of what?" Darcy asks, her eyes shooting to mine.

"In the world of merfolk," he repeats as though he's just said something totally normal, like "in an apartment downtown," but in reality, what he said is the complete opposite of normal.

"Merfolk. As in . . . *mermaids*?" I manage to ask, even though I really don't want to know the answer. I'm pretty darn sure all my hopes with this guy have just been dealt a *Game of Thrones*-scale deathblow.

He nods. "Mermaids, mermen, merboys, and mergirls. We're a community, people coming together from all walks of life in the merfolk lifestyle." He places his hand on mine. "I really hope it's something that resonates with you, Sophie. Perhaps all of you."

Jason puts his hand up in the air. "Oh, I'm definitely in on this."

That strange Darryl Hannah comment about growing my hair suddenly makes sense. He wants me to be a mermaid with him, "living the merfolk lifestyle!"

This cannot be happening. The cute guy from High Tea who seemed to have it all going on, the guy with his head screwed on right, who loves his mom is a freaking *merman*?

No, just *no*.

I think I've burst a blood vessel in my brain.

"You'd make an amazing mermaid, Sophie," he continues, gazing at me as he takes a strand of my hair in his hand.

I'm too stunned to respond. Instead, I simply gawp at him as though . . . well, as though he's just told me he's a merman.

"Okay, explain something to me here, Dave," Jason begins. "You like to swim around dressed up as a fish with a bunch of other people, also dressed up like fish, and do what? Commune with sea life? Braid seaweed together? What?"

Jason's tone isn't lost on David. He might be a wannabe merman, but he's not stupid. "I get it. This is new to you. A lot of people have this reaction when they hear about my merfolk lifestyle."

I swear, if he says, "merfolk lifestyle" one more time, I may blow enough blood vessels to render my brain completely useless.

"So, you're trying to be Aquaman?" This from an amused and persistent Jason.

David shakes his (human) head. "Oh, no. Aquaman's not a merman. And anyway, he's not real."

"Jason Momoa is though," the Momoa-obsessed Darcy comments.

"Aquaman's not real but *mermen* are real?" Jason is trying to suppress his grin—and barely managing it.

"Look, I know you're finding this hard to get your head around. But did you know that for thousands of years, many cultures around the globe have had stories of merfolk? Many, many cultures, not just one or two. Coincidence? I think not."

"Back up the bus here," Darcy says. "You're telling us that not only do you 'live the merfolk lifestyle,' but you believe they exist, too?"

"Well, yes," David replies as though it's a commonly held truth that half human, half fish creatures swim through our waters every day of the week. "Could all those cultures be wrong?"

Err, yes, David. Yes, they could.

"How do you do it, exactly? How do you swim around dressed as a merman?" Erin asks.

"It's really quite simple. I've got a monofin I use when I swim. It straps around my hips and stays on in the water. It's a work of art, really. So beautiful. It's very freeing to swim with it in place."

"I would have thought it would be the exact opposite of 'freeing,'" Darcy mutters quietly to me.

Erin darts me a quick look before saying, "Right. Well. I, ah, think we've learned quite a lot about you today. Thank you for sharing that with us, David." The ever-tactful Erin gives him a shaky smile.

"I'm always keen to share this part of me with new, open people. I sense some of you might find this a little hard." He looks pointedly at Jason. "But I hope you'll reflect on it and perhaps even consider the lifestyle one day." He puts his hand on mine and gives me a meaningful look.

"Well, I don't know about the rest of us, but I'm guessing that about wraps things up," Darcy says. "Sophie? Any final words?"

Other than "no way, José," nothing. "I'll, ah, see you in a minute? We need to discuss things." I say to him.

He gives my hand a squeeze and stands up. "Is that how this works now? You discuss me, and I see if I passed?"

"Yes. We will see if you passed." Erin does her best to suppress a grin.

Once David's out of earshot, I shake my head, "Oh, my God. Oh, my God. Oh, my God."

"Has that guy watched *The Little Mermaid* one too many times or something?" Erin asks.

"Soph, you've outdone yourself with this one. Your date thinks he's a fish," Darcy manages before her laughter overflows.

"Half fish, half man," Erin corrects, Darcy's laugh catching as she too erupts.

"Imagine if he didn't get the memo on which parts were meant to be fish and which parts were meant to be human. He could turn up to one of these merfolk lifestyle get-togethers with a fish head and human legs." Jason laughs at his own joke, and before long, all four of us are swept up in our laughter together.

I wipe the tears from my eyes. "I don't get it. What's the appeal? You can't move your legs and you've got to spend all your time trying to stay afloat in the water."

"Isn't it obvious?" Jason says. "It's a sex thing. He wants to get it on like he's a fish."

I slap him on the arm. "Jason!"

"Come on. What else can it be? The guy's a marine biologist, he loves marine life, he works in an aquarium; he's got a serious thing for fish."

"Maybe he wants to do it with tuna?" Darcy says.

We continue to laugh as we all come up with increasingly ridiculous jokes about fish, until the fact I've lost another potential date begins to settle into my brain.

Jason's smile is cheeky when he asks, "Where are you going on your first date with him, McCarthy?"

I shoot him a look. "Don't be a jerk, Christie. You know I'm not going to date that guy."

Erin gestures toward the bar where David is still standing, beer in hand, scrolling through his phone. "You'd better go tell him."

I let out a heavy sigh. Telling the guy I'd pinned my hopes on as one of the non-weird, non-jerk variety that it's not going to work out between us is not the way I saw this evening going.

I approach him at the bar, and he looks up at me with an inquisitive look on his face.

"I'm sorry, David. There's not going to be a first date."

"I get it. It's too much for you."

I press my lips together and nod. What else can I do? He's one hundred percent right.

"You know, you really should give the merfolk lifestyle a chance. I think you'd find it very appealing."

I beg to differ.

"Thanks for putting yourself through this, David. I'm sorry it didn't work out. No hard feelings?"

He touches his fingertips to my hair once more. "Grow it. You'll look sensational. And yes, no hard feelings."

That night, after an inevitable string of merman jokes from Jas, I climb into my bed and pull the covers over my head. A large, heavy brick settles in my belly as a feeling of hopelessness washes through me.

Merfolk and feeders. *Way to go, Sophie.*

Will I ever find a decent guy to date?

Chapter 15

I plod down the hallway toward the kitchen in my bare feet, hoping Jason is still asleep. The gods seem to be against me in all things these days, so I'm barely surprised when I spot him making a pot of coffee in the kitchen.

He turns to face me, coffee pot and mug in hand. "You don't look set to join the 'merfolk lifestyle' this morning, McCarthy. Shall I go get your monofin for you?"

I shake my head and let out a defeated sigh. What made me clutch my sides in laughter last night lands like a lead balloon today.

There's no use pretending. I'd lain awake half the night, dramatic thoughts like "there are no good guys left in the world" and "I'll never fall in love" and my personal favorite, "I was born alone and I will die alone," rolled through my mind like deafening and persistent thunder.

"Don't. I had a crappy night, and I fully expect to have a crappy day. I don't know why I agreed to do a shift at the café today." I nod at the coffee. "Is that for me?"

"It can be." He pours some coffee into the mug and passes it to me. "The milk is already in there."

I take it in my hands. "Awesome." I take my first sip as I sink down onto one of our two kitchen stools. "It's good. Thanks."

"Well, drink up. With a shift at the café to get to, you'll need to be caffeinated to the gills." His face creases into a smile once he realizes his fish reference has gone down like an oyster. I hate oysters. "Sorry. That wasn't intentional."

"But last night's endless quips were?"

"The guy's a merman, Soph. A *merman*."

Maybe it's the caffeine hitting my bloodstream, or maybe I'm delirious from the potent combination of feeling depressed and a lousy sleep, but a giggle builds up inside me until it bursts out, sending my mouthful of coffee both up my nose and out onto the counter in front of me.

So ladylike. Mom would be proud.

Jason furrows his brow as he chuckles. "There's no need to spurt a perfectly good cup of coffee around the kitchen, McCarthy. Here." He hands me a paper towel and I pat myself down and then the counter.

I rub my nose. "Oh, that hurts."

"Well, as a doctor, I have it on good authority that coffee is designed to go *down* the esophagus and *into* the stomach, rather than *up* through the nasal cavity and *out* through the nose." He uses useful hand gestures to illustrate his point.

"You're a genius then, aren't you?" I give my face one more wipe before balling the paper towel up. "And you're an almost-doctor, not the real deal."

He shrugs. "Semantics, McCarthy. Semantics. I'm not the one redecorating the kitchen with coffee shot from out of my nose right now."

I lift the coffee mug to my lips and pause. "Don't say anything funny for the next five seconds, okay? I need this caffeine in my bloodstream to face my day."

He mimes zipping his mouth up, attaching a padlock, locking it, then placing the key in his jeans pocket.

I shake my head. "You're such a dork, Christie." I take a sip of my coffee and close my eyes as I let the warm liquid slide down my throat. When I open my eyes again, Jason has a concerned look on his face.

"Permission to unzip?" he asks out of the corner of his mouth with his teeth clamped together.

I nod.

"Good, because not being able to talk has got to be the worst torture." He pours himself a mug of coffee then comes to sit next to me at the counter. "Okay, spill. Is this all about Davy Crockett of the fish-loving merfolk?"

I let out a heavy sigh, incapable of smiling. "Him, Andrew, Oliver. There must be a decent guy out there for me to date. And you know what? That's all I need: one normal, nice, decent, non-weirdo guy. Is that too much to ask?"

"Apparently, it is, if the last handful you've picked are anything to go by."

"Maybe it's me? Maybe I attract the weirdos? And no jokes," I warn. "I can't take you ribbing me this morning." I drop my head and feel the cool kitchen counter under my forehead.

"Listen up, McCarthy. It's not you. No way. You're one cool chick. You're just having a bad run, that's all. We all have them."

I raise my head a few inches from the counter to look at him. "Don't tell me there's trouble in doctors and nurses paradise?"

He shrugs. "No trouble. My point is, it's just a frustrating phase. Nothing more. And believe me when I say there's absolutely nothing wrong with you."

"There's nothing wrong with me? Jason Christie, you sweet talker. No wonder you get so many dates." I straighten back up and take another sip of my coffee. A girl can only rest her head on a kitchen counter for so long before it becomes tragic. And I don't want to be tragic.

"You know what I mean. You'll find the right guy for you. You know what they say, he'll turn up when you least expect it."

"And until then, I get to enjoy my boyfriend-less existence, running a business that's losing customers, with pressure from my family to 'do something important' with my life. Cool."

"Now you're sounding like a total drama queen, McCarthy."

"I know." I slump my shoulders. "I don't mean to sound dramatic. It's just that Sean and the others agreed to give me eight months to make something of my new job at High Tea, and Bailey's been telling me it's losing customers and she doesn't know why. Jas, if High Tea goes out of business, I could end up as an unpaid intern, living in my old bedroom in my parents' house until I'm, like, forty. With no dates!"

"We'll have to do something about the terrible state of your life, then, won't we?"

"Any suggestions? I'm open to everything."

"Well, first up, I suggest you finish your coffee, taking extra care *not* to snort it up your nose. Then, have a shower, go to work, and figure things out with Bailey. You're a smart girl, I know you can do this."

"You make it sound so easy."

"It is easy. And Soph? You've got this."

As our gazes lock, I notice for the first time that his brown eyes have flecks of gray and gold. It gives them a certain depth and makes them sparkle.

Strange. I've never noticed that before.

The skin around the edges of his eyes begins to crinkle as a warm smile grows on his face, and a sense of hope builds inside me for the first time since before the David 'merfolk lifestyle' debacle last night.

I square my shoulders. "Yeah, you're right, Jas. I do. I've got this."

"That's the Sophie McCarthy I know and love."

I swallow the last of my coffee and climb down from the stool. I begin to make my way down the hallway to my room, when I stop, turn back, and say, "Thanks, Jas. You're the best."

He gives a self-deprecating shrug. "It's all purely selfish, you know. I don't want my roomie moping around all day, and I definitely don't want to have to replace her if she moves back to live with her parents."

I let out a laugh as I resume walking to my room. "You're so predictable, Christie."

DURING MY COMMUTE into the Cozy Cottage, which involves me sitting in a long stream of traffic and occasionally crawling through the streets of Auckland, I push obsessing over my inability to meet a nice, normal guy to the back of my head. What's the point in beating myself up about it? Jason's right, one hundred percent. There *are* great guys out there. I've just got to stop looking and one will appear.

Maybe I can magic him up?

Ha! If only.

I turn my mind to High Tea's lack of customers. As I wait behind an SUV at my fifth set of red traffic lights so far, I drum my fingers against the steering wheel. I need to find a fix. Bailey said she had no idea why the customer numbers had been falling, and on the surface at least, it's not at all obvious. One thing I know for sure is it's not the quality of the food. Bailey and Paige are fantastic cooks, and the Cozy Cottage Café is famous throughout the city for its delicious cakes. But, at the risk of sounding like a cross between Sean and Yoda: cake does not a high tea make.

I pull into my parking space and take the short walk to the café. It's Friday morning, and I'm pulling a super lengthy one at the café today. Friday nights have long been the Cozy Cottage Friday Night Jam, with local musician performances each week and an open mic night once a month. They're a lot of fun and a lot of work.

I push through the door to the kitchen and am immediately greeted by the aroma of freshly baked cakes. Bailey turns and greets me with a bright "Hello" accompanied by a beaming smile, oven gloves on her hands as she transfers a freshly baked chocolate cake to the counter.

There are some major perks to working at the Cozy Cottage.

"Thank you so much for agreeing to do this long shift today, Sophie. You're a total lifesaver, and I'm going to pay you double for tonight."

"Thanks! I could do with the cash." I pull a laundered Cozy Cottage Café polka dot apron from under the kitchen counter and slip it over my head. "I love the open mic night. You never know what's going to play out in front of your eyes."

"Like Marissa singing a love song to win Nash's love?"

I place my hand over my heart. "Oh, that was so romantic."

Bailey lets out a sigh. "I know. My sister-in-law knows how to pull off a super grand gesture, that's for sure. Speaking of romance, you went on a date with a new guy, didn't you? That guy from High Tea?"

An image of David wearing a monofin and a Davy Crocket-style hat pops into my head, and my insides twist. "It didn't work out."

She pulls out another cake from the oven and places it on the counter next to the chocolate cake. "That's a shame. Was it the vetting or did you just not click?"

"It was more his lifestyle. He told us all about it during the Vetting Process. He's a merman."

"A mer what?"

"A merman. It's the male equivalent of a mermaid."

Surprise registers on her face. "Oh."

"Oh exactly. Not my thing. So," I say with a sigh, "I'm back to boring old single Sophie."

"You're never boring, Sophie." She puts her hands on her hips and bites her lip, clearly pondering something. "What about that cute guy that comes in here all the time?"

"You may need to be a little more specific, Bailey."

"He's tall, broad, got dark hair, and wears a suit and glasses all the time. He's clean-cut but with a sporty edge. Looks like Clark Kent, remember?"

"Oh, yeah. Clark Kent." I visualize the guy with ease. I admit, I have noticed him before. What woman wouldn't? With his tall, athletic physique and handsome features, he looks like a superhero in a suit, ready for action. It would be hard *not* to notice a guy like him. We've shared smiles and light conversation as I've made him coffee before, but it's never gone anywhere.

"I wonder if he's got his Lycra suit under his clothes?"

I raise my eyebrows. "Bailey Jones, you're a married woman."

"Oh, I know, a very happily married woman at that. I wouldn't switch Ryan for any man on this sweet earth. But a woman can *notice* things, can't she?"

"I guess."

"He's hot, though, right?"

"Do the Irish eat potatoes? Of course he's hot! But Bailey, whether he's hot or not isn't the point. I'm no Lois Lane."

"Oh, you're much cuter than Lois Lane, honey. You should chat to him when he's in next." She picks up a fully frosted carrot cake and walks toward the café, pausing near me to add, "Which I bet will be today."

As I collect the keys from the hook by the door and follow her out into the café, I'm not exactly feeling like putting myself out there with some new guy. My track record since starting the No More Bad Dates Pact has not been something to brag about, and I'm not sure I want to get my hopes up with some other guy, even if he masquerades as Clark Kent.

I pull the front door open and come face to face with a guy maybe a couple of years older than me, his hand raised in a fist to tap on the door. He's wearing a pair of jeans and a plain navy T-shirt, his wavy brown hair pushed behind his ears.

My jaw drops open as recognition hits me between the eyes. "Alex?"

His handsome face creases into a grin. "Sophie McCarthy!" He collects me in a hug, lifting me right off the ground. "I had no idea you worked here."

"It's your lucky day, then. Isn't it?" I tease.

"Or maybe it's yours. I'm working here now, too."

I raise my eyebrows at him. "What happened to the great photography career? I thought you were off traveling the globe, snapping photos, and living the high life."

"Traveling the globe, snapping photos, yes. Living the high life? Well, I'm here to work as a barista. Is that 'high life' enough for you?"

"Do you two know each other?" Bailey says as she walks across the café toward us.

I grin at Alex and turn to Bailey. "Alex is my cousin."

"Sort-of cousin," he corrects. "We could never quite work it out."

"His mom is my mom's aunt. She had kids a lot later than my mom, which is why Alex is only two years older than me," I explain unnecessarily. Really, calling Alex my cousin is where I should have left it for simplicity's sake.

"Well, welcome to the Cozy Cottage Café, Sophie's almost cousin. I had no idea you were related when I interviewed you last week." Bailey extends her hand and Alex shakes it.

"Thanks, Bailey. I promise not to give her any noogies while I work here, despite the fact she's my annoying younger cousin."

I laugh. "Oh, you were good at the noogies. It didn't help that you were always so much bigger than me."

"Come with me, Alex. I'll get you all set," Bailey says.

As customers begin a slow but steady stream through the door, Bailey takes Alex out to the kitchen, and I greet a couple of our regulars as I begin my barista tasks for the day.

"Bailey didn't mention an Alex Walsh was starting here today, huh?"

I look up from my jug of frothy milk at Alex. He's standing behind the counter, still with that familiar grin plastered across his face, only this time he's got his hair tied back and is wearing a frilly pink Cozy Cottage Café apron wrapped around his middle.

"Nice apron. The pink really brings out the color of your eyes."

"I'm secure enough in my manhood to wear pink, you know."

"I don't want to hear about your manhood, thanks." I chuckle. "What are you doing here, anyway? You're a big deal photographer not a lowly barista like me."

"Don't put yourself down, Soph. That's my job."

"Is that right? Still with the banter, huh?"

"Hey, remember when we were kids and you used to turn up at our house in your pretty princess dresses and I'd make you play war?"

I smile at the memory. "I'd always end up covered in mud, and Mom would be furious with me when it came time to go home."

"But it was fun, right?"

"Totally."

"Well, imagine here at the café, I'm the one in the pretty princess dress and you're the one getting me to play war."

"I'm not sure I follow."

"Just show me what to do."

"It'll be my pleasure." I grin at my cousin.

This is exactly what I need. Someone to mix it up with, to take my mind off of dating disasters and High Tea problems.

Maybe my day is looking up, after all?

Chapter 16

Since my usual Saturday night karaoke plans have been smashed by a Mandatory McCarthy Meal, Erin and Darcy have come to the open mic night at the Cozy Cottage Café to sing. I'm self-aware enough about my singing abilities that I agreed *not* to sing with them when they take on "Mama Mia" tonight at my place of work. I may love to sing, but it doesn't love me back. And I'm okay with that. Well, as okay as a frustrated pop diva with zero actual talent can be.

And besides, I need this job, and I'm pretty darn sure me performing could seriously compromise that.

Unsurprisingly, my friends were more than happy to accept my "I've got to work" excuse, and they're now sitting together at one of the tables with Jason and Ski Jump Nose—sorry, I mean *Megan*—a mere two performances away from their three minutes of fame. Well, three minutes of Cozy Cottage Open Mic fame, anyway.

Jason comes over to where I'm standing by the register and places his elbow on the counter as he watches the performer on the tiny stage. He leans in closer to me and says loud enough so I can hear him over the music, "It won't be the same without you slaughtering the song up there with the girls, you know."

I feign offense. "Thanks a lot! But we all know they're better off without me. And I don't want everyone here knowing my musical talents are, well, nonexistent."

He shoots me his trademark cheeky grin. "That's not true. You're out of tune and miss the melody most of the time, but at least you know the words."

I hit him on the arm, possibly a little too hard when he exclaims, "Ow!"

"Sorry, not sorry?" I give him my most innocent smile and bat my eyelashes at him.

He rubs his arm. "Yeah, I'm sure you are."

"I see Megan's still on the scene." I nod in her direction. She's leaning across the table, listening to something Darcy's saying. "She looks gorgeous tonight in that dress, her long blonde hair falling around her shoulders. Hey," I begin as a thought occurs to me, "with hair like that, I bet David would like her. She's got definite mermaid potential."

"I'll be sure to mention the 'merfolk lifestyle' to her. She's excited about tonight. She loves an open mic night."

"That's right, she's a Von Trapp."

"Only without the Nazis, remember?"

We share a smile, and I'm struck by how easy things are between the two of us. It's always been this way, from the moment we met. Why can't things be easy and fun like that with the guys I'm trying to date?

Seriously, should it be this hard?

"Have you put any more thought into what to do about High Tea?" Jason asks.

"Actually, I have. I spent some time on the web today, doing some research. I've got some ideas I'm beginning to put together, but I need to visit the competition first."

"That sounds promising."

I bite my lip when I think of what's at stake. "It needs to be. I've got to keep this job, Jas."

"Well, you've definitely made the right call in not singing tonight then," he replies, his eyes sparkling. "That's a good start."

"I'd love to disagree with you, but I can't."

Alex walks out of the kitchen with plates stacked up his arms. He grins and winks at me as he passes by, and I beam back at him.

"New server?" Jason asks.

"Yup. He started today."

Jason nods as he eyes Alex up across the café. "What's he like?"

"Oh, Alex is the best. He's funny and clever. He's a photographer, you know. A really good one."

He narrows his eyes at me. "You like him, huh?"

I can tell Jason's got his hackles up. I'm not sure why, but I like the idea of teasing him about Alex. "Who wouldn't? I mean, look at the guy. He's tall and totally built. I bet he'd look good in . . . well, anything, really."

We both watch as Alex places the final plate in front of a woman who looks up adoringly at him. Alex has always had women throwing themselves at him, ever since he sprouted his shoulders and long legs as a fifteen-year-old kid. Sure, he's good looking, anyone can see that, but there's something more to him, a charm, charisma. Call it what you like, Alex Walsh has it in spades.

He strides around the back of the counter and winks at me once more. "Next load."

Once he's disappeared out back, Jason says, "You're not lining him up for a date, are you?"

"Why do you ask?"

He tries a nonchalant shrug. "No reason. I just wondered, that's all."

"Let's assess him, shall we?" I lean my elbows on the counter and start counting off on my fingers. "Is he single? Check. Is he in the target age-range? Check. Is he good looking? Double check. Really, Jas, I see no reason why I shouldn't pursue an Initial Contact with Alex."

"How do you know he's not into freaky stuff? Have you forgotten all about the merman? Really, Soph, I would have expected you'd have waited more than a measly twenty-four hours before you launched yourself at some other guy."

Affronted, I stand up straight and glare at him, "I'm not *launching* myself at anyone, thank you very much."

He cocks an eyebrow. "Oh yeah? What about Alex?"

I give a bitter laugh. I was on the verge of telling Jason that Alex and I are cousins—okay, sort-of cousins—and consequently of no interest to me as potential date material. I've changed my mind. Whatever bee has got under his bonnet, I'm going to leave it there to buzz around for a while. Who knows? Maybe it'll even give him a good sting?

I cross my arms, defensive. "Isn't that the whole point of the pact? To find Mr. Right for Now? I've got to at least try to date."

"Maybe let the paint dry on the merman first, huh?"

I narrow my eyes at him. "Why do you care if I want to go out with someone else, anyway?"

It's a very good question, and one I'd really rather like to know the answer to. One minute he's all gung-ho about me dating, and now he's treating me like some sort of desperate cheerleader on the prowl at prom.

He simply shrugs. "No reason. I'm just looking out for you, that's all. We're buds."

Cue feeling bad.

He's right; we are buds. Best buds. Only just this morning he had been an amazing friend to me, telling me not to get upset about things not working out with David, encouraging me to find a solution to High Tea's financial woes. Really, whatever's behind the way he's acting over Alex tonight, I should let it fly.

Jason deserves more from me.

"Okay, full disclosure," I begin.

He puts his hands up in the air. "If this is about how you want to do illicit things with that new guy, I really, *really* don't want to hear it."

I shake my head. "I'm not going on a date with Alex Walsh now or at any time."

I think I detect a hint of a relieved smile on his face, but I might be reading too much into it. I've done it before.

"Why not?" he questions.

"He's my cousin, and this isn't *Game of Thrones*."

Jason's eyes bulge. "He's your cousin? Well, why didn't you say so?"

I lift a shoulder.

"Alex Walsh, huh? He seems like a great guy."

I let out an exasperated laugh at his whiplash-inducing change of opinion. "You're impossible. Do you know that, Christie?"

"That's *Doctor* Jason Christie to you."

I roll my eyes. "We've been over this. You're a trainee doctor, remember?"

"Not for much longer. I'm officially a fully-fledged M.D. next month."

"Seriously? Jas, that's awesome!" I round the counter and give him a hug. "With you finally an actual doctor, my life is going to be thoroughly miserable, isn't it?"

"If you mean miserable for you but fantastic for your fully-fledged doctor roommate? Then yes, it is. And I'm going to enjoy every last minute of it."

I laugh as I release him from the hug and place my hand on his shoulder. "Moving back in with my parents to take that internship has never looked so appealing."

"Now I know you're kidding."

Alex stops beside us. "No one needs to see their cousin making out, you know. Go get a room, you two."

We leap back from one another like we've both been electrocuted. A loud, surprised laugh escapes my lips. "We're not making out," I explain as Jason says, "That's not what this is, man."

Alex's eyes dart between us. "Sure. Whatever you say, guys."

"No, seriously. We're roommates. That's all," I say hurriedly. "This is Jason Christie. Jason, this is my cousin, Alex Walsh."

The men shake hands. "Hey, man. Great to meet Sophie's roommate," Alex says.

"You, too," Jason says. "I didn't know you existed until a couple minutes ago."

"I didn't know *you* existed until just about five seconds ago," Alex replies with a wicked grin.

"Well, I guess we're both in the same boat then. Sophie hasn't mentioned either of us."

"Sure. Something like that."

It's like watching a couple of sparring knights use blunt wooden swords so all they can do is prod each other. It's strange and a little confusing, but I'll admit, it's also pretty darn funny.

Jason's the one who breaks the tension. "I guess it doesn't matter, does it? It's good to meet you, man."

Just then, Bailey walks past us, and I touch her on the arm to get her attention. "Bailey, can I talk to you for a minute?"

"Sure thing." She nods at Jason in recognition and says to Alex, "I think table five wants to place an order. They've got menus."

"I'm on it, boss," Alex replies with a grin and a mock salute, and I'm certain I hear the women at the table beside us collectively sigh.

Once out in the kitchen, Bailey leans against the counter and asks, "What's up?"

I'm going out on a limb here, so although I think I'm onto something with my thoughts around High Tea, I'm suddenly nervous. "You know how you mentioned High Tea's falling customer numbers? Well, I wondered if you'd be okay with me putting a proposal together."

"A proposal to help lift the numbers? Of course! We're totally open to your ideas."

"Awesome. I'll need to have a better look at the spreadsheet you showed me the other day, too. I'd like to get a clear understanding of where the business sits."

"Oh." Bailey's uncertain expression tells me I've got to give her more.

"You might not know that I graduated at the top of my finance class a few years back. I'm sorry if I sound like I'm bragging. I'm not, honestly. That's not what this is about. I just figure I may be able to help. I guess I just 'get' numbers."

Unlike men, who I definitely do not get—even my roommate and cousin now, if the bizarre sparring I witnessed is anything to go by.

Bailey's face lights up. "Of course you can see the numbers. You are the Weekend Manager now. I'll email it to you when I'm home tonight."

"Thanks. I've already got some ideas."

"You do? I'd love to hear them."

"They're still percolating, like a cup of Ned's coffee."

She smiles. "You're all about tea these days, remember?"

"Oh, but I do love my coffee."

A few moments later, I'm back out in the café where Erin and Darcy are already up on the makeshift stage, preparing to sing. Jason is back at the table, sitting with Megan.

I sidle up to Alex, who's holding some used crockery in his hands. I nod at the stage and say with pride, "My BFFs are about to sing."

"They're your friends?" Alex asks.

"Yup. The taller one with the long dark hair is Darcy, and the other one is Erin. They were in high school with us, but I guess that was a long time ago now. They're going to sing 'Mama Mia.'"

Alex nods as he watches the girls on the makeshift stage. "Going retro. I like it."

As they kick their vocals off, the audience applauds and claps along to the familiar tune. And they're good. Dressed in cute '70's belted tunics Erin designed and sewed herself, they look every inch the pop divas they should have been. Maybe in another lifetime.

ALEX and I bob our heads to the music, and I grin as I watch my girls looking so amazing up there. I glance over at Jason and Megan at the table. He's got his arm slung around the back of her chair, beaming at Megan who's jiggling her pert little butt in her seat to the music. They look like the perfect couple; young, good looking, happy, in love.

For some reason I don't understand, my insides twist at the sight of them.

The girls sing their last note and lean their backs against one another, á la Agnetha and Frida themselves. I applaud enthusiastically along with the rest of the audience. The girls beam out at us all and then take a bow and return to their seats, making way for the next performer. There's always a rush on orders between songs so I get less than thirty seconds to congratulate my friends before I'm needed.

"Who's the new server?" Darcy asks as she takes her seat. "He looks familiar."

"We've decided he's definitely date-worthy," Erin adds. "Are you sizing him up as a potential?"

I shake my head. "He's my cousin, Alex Walsh. Remember him? He was at school with us, two years ahead."

Darcy guffaws. "*That's* Alex Walsh?" I give an amused nod, and Darcy's eyes get huge. "Well, didn't he grow up."

"He grew up g*ooood*." Erin mock-fans her face as both my friends watch Alex saunter back to the kitchen.

Really, they're acting like a couple of dogs in heat.

Jason eyes Erin and Darcy across the table. "So, let me get this straight: everyone's got a thing for Sophie's cousin now, have they?"

"I don't," Megan says as she wraps herself around one of Jason's arms. "I've got a thing for *you*," she coos.

You know what, Megan? I think we got that.

My BFFs lusting after my cousin is weirding me out enough, but watching Megan fawn over Jason makes me feel strange inside.

It's definitely my cue to leave.

"Okay, people. I'll leave you to your evening." I make my exit.

For the rest of the evening, I return my attention to where it ought to be: my job. I take orders, pour drinks, help deliver meals. But something's stuck in my head, and it's giving me an unsettled feeling in the pit of my stomach.

Although I would never admit it to anyone, I didn't like seeing Jason and Megan together like that.

And for the life of me, I can't work out why.

Chapter 17

I'll admit it. Sitting at the dinner table with my entire family for a Mandatory McCarthy Meal is not at the top of my list of favorite things to do on a Saturday night. Particularly when my decision not to take an internship at either McCarthy & McCarthy Solicitors or Baby-ness is still a big, fat, juicy bone of contention for my well-meaning siblings.

Did I say "well-meaning?" I meant overbearing, all up in my business, go ruin someone else's life siblings.

My bad.

All I can say is I am totally indebted to Jason for offering to come with me to face the wolves. Of course, he assures me his attendance at this Mandatory McCarthy Meal has everything to do with the fact that he adores Mom's homemade bread pudding, but I don't care. Tonight, the first meal since my announcement that I wasn't taking either of the internships, I need as many people in my corner as I can get.

We've managed to get through the entire dinner of lamb stew and mashed potatoes (for a change), and are almost on the home stretch over Mom's carb-tastic bread pudding when Dad innocently asks, "Sophie? How's this brilliant new job of yours working out?"

I love my dad, really I do, but why did he have to go ask that?

I steel myself for the inevitable internship comments and try my best to push from mind the fact that High Tea, and consequently my new job, is in financial straits. "It's awesome, Dad. High Tea is great, being the weekend manager is great, and it's all, well . . . just great."

Dad beams at me. "That's so wonderful, love."

"It *is* wonderful. Thanks, Dad. I made the right decision to take this new and exciting job, and I love being the manager." I look pointedly across the table at Sean and Fiona.

"*Weekend* manager," Sean adds helpfully.

"That's right. The weekends are High Tea's busiest time of the week and represent most of the profits," I reply, trying not to sound too defensive but guessing I probably do.

"She's really very good at what she does, you know," Jason says to Sean. "You should drop in and see for yourself."

I beam at Jason before I turn back to Sean and add, "Although you really should book. We get very busy."

"Oh, good for you, *dote*," Mom says. "Your dad and I knew you'd make a real success of whatever you put your mind to. And you're still working at the café during the week?"

"I am. I get Mondays and Tuesdays off. The way I see it, I get the best of both worlds: High Tea and the Cozy Cottage." I look across the table at Sean, the ringleader, and challenge him to say anything negative about my job in the face of such glowing parental approval.

Sean swallows a mouthful and places his fork on his now empty plate. "Tell me something, Sophie. What's your career path? Where do see yourself in, I don't know, two years, three?"

All eyes at the table turn to me, even baby Lola's and baby Simon's, although I suspect that's mainly because their moms are watching me and not because they're ganging up on me, too.

It's a good question. With Paige back after the babies are born, where *do* I see myself in two years? Although it's suited me just fine so far, I'm not sure I see myself as being a barista when I'm pushing twenty-eight. I chew on my lip as I work out how to answer. After a moment, I begin, "Well, as I said, I really love working at High Tea, so I'd like to still be there. I've got a big opportunity right now. Huge, in fact."

"Doing what?" Fiona asks.

"To show my bosses my worth by improving the customer numbers. I want to make High Tea the best offering of its kind in Auckland city."

Until this moment, I hadn't even worked out that was what I wanted. But suddenly, it all seems so clear: I want to do what I love to do. And I love managing Cozy Cottage High Tea.

I lean back in my seat, confident in my new-found direction in life. It feels good. It feels right. Full-time manager of Cozy Cottage High Tea. I like the sound of that.

I've just got to make it happen.

Caitlin crinkles her brow. "What do you mean 'improve the customer numbers?'"

"Is the business in trouble?" Fiona asks.

"Methink'st this is something to be concerned about," Sean adds.

Uh-oh. It would have been best *not* to have mentioned to my family that High Tea is in trouble.

I was almost home free.

All I can do now is try to gloss over it. "It's no big deal. Really, it's not. Bailey told me the numbers are a little down, that's all."

Try *a lot* down. Like needs open-heart surgery down. And I know. As gut-wrenching as it is, I saw it with my own two eyes. I poured over Bailey's spreadsheet during my breaks today, and let's just say that where High Tea was financially when it first opened and where it is now are two totally different places. Totally different *continents.*

And I've been wracking my brain on how to fix it.

"What's 'a little down?'" Caitlin asks. "No more mashies, sweetie. You've had enough and we don't want sickie baby, do we?" That part is directed at Lola, not me, I'm pretty sure.

"Nothing much. Just a handful less customers than, say, this time last year. I've been looking at solutions, though."

"Really? Like what?" Sean's gaze is intense, and my heart thuds in my ears.

This is not how I saw this conversation going.

"Oh, like, err—" My eyes dart desperately around the faces at the table until they land on Jason's. I know the hopeful, positive look on his face is willing me to come up with the goods, to dazzle my siblings into taking me seriously as a woman of business. But under pressure, I ain't got a whole lot right now.

"I think what Sophie is trying to say is that she's working on some promising ideas, but they're in the embryonic stages right now. Right, Soph?" Jason raises his eyebrows and gives me a small encouraging nod.

"Embryonic. That's right." I nod vehemently, although I've never used such a blatantly medical term in my life. I tap the side of my head. "Still working on it. Comin' up with the goods. I could tell you, but I might have to shoot you all." My forced laugh is brittle.

"You know, Sophie's smart," Jason begins. "She's blessed with a strong McCarthy head on her shoulders. Just like all of you have been, too. Successful lawyers," he gestures at Fiona and Sean, who both sit up a little straighter in their chairs. "A successful marketing manager," he nods at Abigail who smiles back at him. "Successful business owner." This time it's Caitlin's turn. "And lest I forget the two best parents anyone could hope to have, Mama and Poppa McCarthy." My parents puff their chests out and beam at him down the table.

My mouth drops open. This guy could charm John Wayne off his horse!

I look around the table at a family transformed. They fell for Jason's charms the moment he stepped into their lives, and he's weaved his magic with them once more tonight. I am so grateful.

I beam at him across the table. "Thank you," I mouth and am rewarded with a raise of the eyebrows.

"Have faith in her. Just as you have faith in yourselves." Jason looks directly into my eyes and adds, "I know I do."

As I look back at him, something new and unexpected moves in my chest. I'm alarmed when a lump begins to form in my throat and tears sting my eyes. What is happening to me? Why is Jason suddenly having an effect on me?

I find myself gazing at Jason as though he's . . . he's . . . what? Someone I have feelings for? Feelings like . . . love?

Wait, *what?!*

That's ridiculous. Jason is Jason, pure and simple. He's my roommate, my friend. That's all he's ever been—and that's a whole lot.

I can't go having *romantic* feelings about him. That's insane! Insane and weird and wrong and dangerous and oh-so many things.

I blink back my unexpected tears and force myself to look elsewhere. I train my eyes on my family instead. Until I can work out what the heck is happening here, it's a much, *much* safer option not to look anywhere near Jason.

"You know, with speeches like that, you should consider running for office one day, Jason," I say with a laugh.

It doesn't take Einstein to work out I'm making light to ward off the new, surprising emotions churning inside me. When really, what I want to do is pull him close to me and thank him for his undying support. Tell him how much he means to me, from the very bottom of my heart.

Crap crappity crap! What has gotten into me?

That would be crazy. Not to mention send my already heightened sense of vulnerability into orbit.

He smiles. "Maybe one day, Soph."

"You know what? You're right, Jason. We should have more faith in Sophie," Abigail says, almost making me fall off my chair in shock.

"I agree," Caitlin says. "And Lola does, too. Don't you, Lolie?" The one-year-old simply gurgles as some salivary mashed potato dribbles out of her mouth. "Just because she chose not to take one of those internships doesn't mean we shouldn't support her. Well done, Sophie. I have faith in you, too."

"Yes. I have faith in you, Sophie." This from Fiona.

"Well, you know what I think of you, love. I'm very proud of you," Dad says with a wink and a smile.

"See? We believe in you, *mo stoirín*," Mom adds.

I blink at them all as I take it in. "Th-thanks, everyone," I manage, as my throat aches from trying not to cry.

All eyes at the table turn to the only silent member of the family. Sean is sitting with his arms crossed, his face stern, his body rigid. Of all the nuts to crack, Sean has always been the toughest. Sometimes I wonder if it's just habit or something he thinks he's got to do. Whatever the reason behind it, he's now backed into a corner, and he doesn't look happy about it.

Mom's the one to give the prod. "What do you have to say to our Sophie, love?"

He grinds his teeth. Like actually grinds them, as though he's a grumpy cartoon character. "What I have to say is that I hope it all works out the way she wants it to."

"And that you have faith in her," Dad prompts.

When Sean doesn't say anything further, Mom glares at him and says "Love" in the "you'd better do what you're told or else" tone we all knew so well growing up in the McCarthy family household.

"And I have faith in Sophie," Sean pronounces, although his tone and body language tell another story entirely.

I shoot him a triumphant smile.

Sophie: one. Sean: negative three trillion and four.

Lola begins to grizzle, and Caitlin tries to distract her with her keys, which promptly get dispensed to the floor. Before long, she's begun to wail, and Simon joins in.

"Mandatory McCarthy Meals are just not practical for us in the evenings anymore, Mom. Lola's dinnertime is five o'clock, and she needs to be in bed at seven. All this stimulation is going to have her totally wired, and you know what that means." Caitlin shoots us all a meaningful look.

I glance around the table. No one responds. I come up with a few potential outcomes of my own, such as a full-scale toddler revolution, planet Earth spinning off its axis, perhaps the end of humankind as we know it? But I keep schtum. No need to poke the Caitlin-shaped beast over her daughter, especially after all the nice things everyone's said about me tonight.

"She'll be up at four tomorrow morning and be overtired all day," Caitlin finishes for us.

"Oh, we don't want that, *a stór*," Mom coos, as Sean says, "Total disaster for all concerned."

Thankfully, the eardrum-saving decision to go home is made.

As Jason drives us back to our apartment, I grip onto the sides of my seat as I wrestle with these new, shocking feelings I seem to have for him.

I struggle to reason with myself. I probably just read far too much into it all. He was simply being the usual nice and supportive friend he is. Emphasis on the word "friend." I've been having a bad run in the date department, so I got things twisted.

That's all. Nothing more.

Jason's voice punctuates my thoughts, bringing me back to Earth. "Tell me something, McCarthy. What is up with Sean and those weird Shakespearean expressions of his?"

"He likes to think of himself as very learned."

"I've got news: it makes him sound like a dick."

Laugh bubbles up inside me. This. This is what we're good at. Laughing, having fun. *Not* feeling all romantic and mushy about him having faith in me.

"Err, Jas?" I bite my lip. "Thanks for stepping in back there. You really helped me out."

He shrugs, not taking his eyes from the road. "You seemed like you needed help, McCarthy. I love your family, but sometimes they can really get on your case. Especially Sean."

"Tell me about it. Dad's all relaxed and chill, and Sean's like the family patriarch. King Sean, right?"

"All hail King Sean."

"All you minions, do as I say!"

"Maybe he's the Dark Lord, He Who Shall Not Be Named? Or he could be Darth Vader."

I laugh. "Darth's got nothing on Sean."

We fall into silence once more, although this time it feels more like the old Sophie and Jason.

After a couple of blocks, I pluck up the courage to ask, "So, did you just say that thing to help me out?"

"What thing?"

"You know, that thing you said at dinner."

He's going to make me say it, I just know it.

"About how you like bread pudding?"

"Exactly that." My voice drips with sarcasm. "I want to know whether you really meant that you think I like bread pudding. Which, by the way, you already know I do."

"I needed it reconfirmed. It's a big deal to me, you know. I don't think I could be roommates with someone who didn't like Mammy McCarthy's bread pudding."

"You're right. It is a crucial aspect of someone's character."

As we zip through the quiet suburban streets, I go for another shot. "You know, what you said about you having faith in me. Did you mean it?" I hold my breath.

His eyes flash briefly to mine before he returns them to the road. "I meant it."

I can't explain why, but hearing him say those words makes my heart soar. I press my lips together to stop a goofy grin from busting out across my face as I turn to look out the passenger window. "Okay. Well, thanks for that." I aim for an "I'm taking this all in stride" tone but probably hit over-excited Minnie Mouse.

Jason has faith in me, and all is right with the world.

Chapter 18

I wake up the following morning to the sound of birds chirping in the tree outside my window, pleasantly piercing the continual low hum of city traffic. The aroma of freshly brewed coffee wafts through the crack at the bottom of my door, and I breathe it in, savoring the fond thoughts it elicits of the Cozy Cottage, of my friends, of my job.

Of Jason.

I sit bolt upright in my bed.

Jason.

All the conflicting and confusing feelings I've had about him over the last twenty-four hours come crashing back, like a truck smashing through a wall of empty cardboard boxes.

The way he stood up to my family last night in my defense.

The way he told me he had faith in me.

The way he'd looked at me.

I press my lips together to stop a smile in its tracks. Something moves in my chest, all the same.

And then, my mind darts to an earlier image that has my guts twisting: the way he looked with Megan at the Friday Night Jam, all cozied up together and couple-y, like they were made for each other.

I scrunch my eyes shut and shake my head in some sort of deluded attempt to shove the scattered cardboard boxes of feelings into a neat, hidden stack. It's no use. My internal conflict rages, my feelings about Jason becoming more and more confused. Jumbled boxes everywhere.

Why does Jason being with Megan bother me so much? I've seen him with loads of women, all carbon copies of one another: young and pretty, usually nurses or fellow doctors, always totally enamored of him. I've never been bothered by any of them before.

Maybe it's because Megan has stuck around longer than the women in Jason's life usually do? Yes, that's got to be it! I let out a relieved puff of air. Solved it! It's totally clear: I feel weird about him and her together because I don't like Megan.

My fleeting feeling of euphoria evaporates. The problem is, I *do* like her. It's hard not to. She's sweet and kind. There's nothing to dislike.

Then what the heck is it?

A little voice in the back of my head tells me I know exactly what it is.

Only, I thought I was past all that.

Here's the deal. A long time ago, when I first met Jason, I had a bit of a thing for him. I was a fresh-faced graduate, with two and a half boyfriends to my name (the half was due to the fact he lasted less than two weeks, so I didn't think I could count him as a full boyfriend). I responded to Jason's advertisement for a roommate for an inner-city apartment. The place looked ideal, close enough to the Cozy Cottage, in a part of town with plenty of cafés and bars and restaurants nearby.

When we met, I admit I had full-blown symptoms of attraction. You know the ones: elevated heart rate, butterflies batting their wings in my belly, a frankly ludicrous amount of giggling. You get the picture.

Jason was this older, much more worldly guy who knew exactly what he wanted to do with his life and was already going after it. He had charisma that smacked you right between the eyes, plus, there was the small fact that he was better looking than pretty much any guy I'd seen in the flesh before. Call me shallow, but that sure as heck counted.

We hit it off straight away, despite all my incessant giggling, and it came as no surprise when he asked me to be his roommate. I moved in that weekend with the full expectation that a grand romance between us would ensue.

I was wrong.

All too soon, my hopes came crashing down around my ears when he introduced me to his date on my first night in the apartment, a very sweet and pretty nurse. When she was replaced by the next in line and then the next, I made the decision that to keep my sanity, Jason could only ever be a friend. I confided in Darcy and Erin, and they both agreed. Jason was a roommate and a friend. Anything more would only end in heartache for me.

And that approach has worked perfectly for all this time.

And now? Now I'm thoroughly annoyed with myself for allowing past, unreciprocated feelings to grow once more.

I push my hair behind my ears and bite my lip. I know what I need to do. I need to give myself a stern talking to. Tell myself well-considered, logical things. Things like:

1. Jason isn't interested in me romantically
2. We're best friends, and that's more than enough
3. His girlfriends may come and go, but I'm not going anywhere.

There. Done. All I've got to do now is remind myself of these very valid, very true points and the status quo will be preserved.

No more scattered boxes of confusing feelings for Sophie.

Easy peasy.

I push my covers off, swing my legs over the edge of the bed, and stretch. I slip my kimono-style dressing gown on and pad down the hall, lured to the kitchen by the tempting coffee aroma.

A puff of steam wafts out of the bathroom in front of me as Jason steps into the hallway. I stop in my tracks as his eyes land on mine.

Of all the days . . .

"Ah, McCarthy. Top of the mornin' to ya," he says in a terrible rendition of an Irish accent before his face breaks into a totally knee-weakening smile.

"Hey" is about all I can manage as my heart thuds loudly in my ears. I try my level best not to stare at him. And I fail. *Spectacularly.* But come on, people! I've only just started to feel things for this guy again and he turns up looking like he's been photo-shopped to male Adonis perfection, like Ryan Gosling in *Crazy Stupid Love.* The key difference is he's here, right in front of me in the flesh, wearing nothing but a towel. Let me repeat that.

Nothing.

But.

A.

Towel.

That's right, the guy I'm trying super hard to shake some thoroughly inappropriate feelings for is naked but for a piece of material loosely wrapped around his middle. His washboard abs, broad shoulders, and muscular arms are highlighted by glistening pearls of water scattered across his beautiful skin.

Come on!

I glance skyward. *What are you trying to do to me?*

Really, it's a testament to my steely resolve that I don't swoon in front of him, right here and now.

Sure, I've seen him in not much before. He spends summer in shorts and a tank, sometimes shirtless when we're at the beach. But this feels different. It *is* different.

And I don't like it one little bit.

I swallow, hard, and force myself to tear my eyes away. It takes a Herculean effort, but I manage it. Just.

If they were giving out medals for self-control, I'd get a big, shiny gold one with the words "First Rate Kicker of Jason Christie-Related Temptation" emblazoned on it for what I've just achieved.

He cocks an eyebrow, his eyes narrowed. "You okay, McCarthy?"

I clear my throat. "Yes, fine. Just woke up, that's all." I aim for a nonchalant shrug.

"Well, the coffee's in the pot. Go help yourself. I'm gonna go get dressed."

Yes! Get dressed! Put that Jason lusciousness under as many layers of fabric as you can find. Layer it up. Undershirts, over shirts, sweatshirts. Every kind of shirt you can imagine. And when you think you're done, add another stack for good measure. I'm thinking Joey on *Friends*, wearing every item of clothing in Chandler's closet.

Yes. That ought to do it.

"Err, okay." I take a step closer to him so I can get past and he stands back for me.

Hot *and* a gentleman? Seriously?

"Pour me a mug. 'Kay?"

As I slink past him, I hold my breath to stop myself breathing in his scent like some kind of stalker. "You got it, roomie!" I reply in a super light and breezy way.

I reach the safety of the kitchen and bury my face in my hands. Why today? Why? Has someone up there got it in for me? Are they, in all their mysterious wisdom, trying to force me to grow the seed of my feelings for him? To make me want him more? To *torture* me with this?

Of all the days in the hundreds and hundreds of days we've been roommates, to run into him wearing just his towel and a knee-weakening smile, it had to be today? Darcy will be so pleased, her prediction I'd get a Jason eyeful one day come to life.

I let out a sigh as I pull a couple of mugs out of the cupboard and pour some coffee into each one. I add enough milk to cool mine down to an easy drinking temperature and down the whole thing before Jason arrives back in the kitchen. Call me a coward, but until I can get on top of these feelings for him once more—and vanquish that image of his perfect, wet torso—avoiding Jason Christie has got to be my best move.

"OOOH, look at this, Darce. They've got caviar blinis!"

Darcy pulls a face. "Caviar whats?"

I peer over the top of my menu. "Blinis. I think they're like little pancakes. Blini sounds so ritzy, doesn't it? We definitely need to try them."

Darcy and I are sitting in large, comfortable armchairs at a table with a crisp white tablecloth. Soft piano music fills the air, and the atmosphere is one of elegant refinement.

Darcy's concentrating on her menu. "Let's do the high tea that comes with champagne, okay?"

"Don't you have to work this afternoon? I didn't think celebrities took too kindly to their personal assistants turning up drunk in the afternoons."

Darcy waves her hand in the air. "Work schmork. Ingrid will survive without me for a couple hours, and I'll only have a glass."

I beam at her. "Consider my rubber arm duly twisted. Champagne high tea it is."

A few moments later, we place our order with our server, thankful our glasses of champagne are delivered almost immediately. I lean back in my seat and study the room. With its soft, high-backed seating, grand chandeliers hanging from the ceiling, and sweeping opaque curtains framing the windows, this place could not be more different from Cozy Cottage High Tea's relaxed, homey vibe.

"You look like you're taking mental notes," Darcy says.

"That's the whole point. I need to check out the competition, see what they've got that we don't. Look." I gesture around the room. "Every table is full on a Monday. Every single one. Cozy Cottage High Tea isn't even open today."

"Girl, that's a good thing. Otherwise you couldn't be here with me." She raises her champagne flute and we clink glasses.

"I'm checking out what sort of customers come here. There are the ladies who lunch over there," I nod at a group of well-to-do looking older women, dressed almost exclusively in Chanel, "to business people," I nod at a table of men and women in suits, "to, well, us."

"The ones who really can't afford to do this, you mean. Why aren't you open on Mondays?"

"Paige and Bailey think people only want high tea Wednesday through Sunday."

Darcy gestures at the room. "Clearly, they're wrong."

Our server materializes at our table, holding a tiered cake stand full of delicious bite-sized treats. She places it on the table and we thank her.

Darcy surveys the stack of deliciousness in front of us. Everything is exquisitely made, from the small tartlets, topped with pretty flowers, to the caviar blinis and smoked salmon rolls. "This looks amazing."

My mouth waters, right on cue. "Oh, it does." I shoot her a quick smile. "Two, four, six, eight, dig in, don't wait."

Darcy rolls her eyes. "I can't believe you said that in a fancy place like this."

"I guess I'm trying to lighten the mood. It's very quiet and refined here, don't you think?"

"Maybe people like that? I mean, high tea isn't like going to a regular old coffee house, is it?"

"It is at Cozy Cottage High Tea." I chew on my lip as Darcy's observation rolls through my mind.

She puts one of the caviar blinis in her mouth. "Holy crap, this is good!" she announces, her voice loud enough to attract attention from a couple of the nearby tables.

I widen my eyes at her. "Shhh, Darce. People are looking at us."

She swallows her mouthful and leans closer to me. "That's because this place is so stuffy and everyone's too freaking scared to talk louder than a whisper. You'd think we were in the presence of royalty or something."

I scan the room.

An older lady in a pants suit raises her eyebrows at me before she turns back to her equally pant-suited friend.

I shoot her an apologetic smile.

Darcy's right. No one is talking at normal volume. They're all behaving in a formal and polite manner. It's almost like being at St.

Peter's with my family, only with significantly better food. No offense, Father Jarrod.

"You know what? You're totally right, Darce. I feel like we need to be on our best behavior here. It's like we can't be us."

"Exactly," she says, her mouth full of tartlet.

Together, we get stuck into enjoying the delicacies, the champagne, and even the pot of tea. My conversion from coffee addict to tea connoisseur is gaining ground, but it's still a work in progress, that's for sure.

"What's happening on the date front? Have you got your eye on anyone new? I've got zero prospects, and it's starting to depress me." She selects one of the mini cupcakes from the top tier of the cake stand.

My mind instantly darts to Jason in his towel in the hallway this morning, and my belly does an involuntary flip-flop. "No one," I reply without looking her in the eyes.

I pretend I'm concentrating hard on my next selection.

"Are you sure?" she asks, her tone suggesting I've failed to convince her.

Damn my inability to lie effectively!

I shoot her a breezy smile. "Of course I'm sure. Why wouldn't I be?"

She narrows her eyes at me, and I avert my own as I squirm in my chair. "Because you're blushing and you're finding it hard to look at me. Come on, Soph, spill."

I aim for a nonchalant shrug. "There's nothing to spill. Have you tried these mini cupcakes? I think they're chocolate mud." I pop one in my mouth, and add, "They're so good."

"Sophie McCarthy, I know you, and I know full well when you've got something to hide. If you don't tell me, I'll go on the search and find out anyway. You should save us all some time and tell me everything right now."

My sigh is resigned. Darcy is famous among our friends for her sleuth skills. The last thing anyone wants is to have Darcy Evans on their case.

"If I tell you something, you can't make a big deal about it, got it?"

She nods, her eyes bright in anticipation of new and possibly scintillating information. "Tell me everything."

I clasp my hands together as I work out what to say. "First up, I think it's only temporary."

Darcy gives me an encouraging nod. "Only temporary. Got it."

"It'll pass and I'll look back and laugh at how silly I was."

If I were truly honest with myself, as in totally, completely, no holds barred honest, I'd have to say I'm not too sure quite how "temporary" my feelings for Jason are. I mean, he's one of my favorite people. Maybe it's a natural progression for us? Maybe it's even meant to be?

Wait, *what?* Have I gone *insane?*

I swallow down my nerves and try my best to push such outlandish thoughts away. Of course it's temporary. As temporary as a pimple at the end of your nose. It may feel like it's going to be there, tormenting you forever, but it only lasts a few days, and then you're like, "what pimple?" #AlreadyMovedOn.

"Sophie, so far all you've said is that it's temporary. Are you going to elaborate, or should I play the 'guess what's eating Sophie McCarthy' game?" Darcy raises her eyebrows in expectation.

"Look, before I say anything more, I know it's a really, really bad idea, and I'm never ever going to do anything about it."

"Ok*aaay.*"

"Also, I need to say that I really think that—"

"Soph?" she interrupts, "Just spit it out."

Before I have the chance to wimp out, I scrunch my eyes shut and blurt, "Jason. I've started to feel things for Jason." I open my eyes a fraction and see Darcy's hand fly to her mouth, her already big brown eyes so huge, she looks like a puppy begging for food.

When she fails to respond to my declaration, I place my elbows on the table and lean closer to her. "Aren't you going to say anything?"

She lowers her hand and clears her throat. "I owe Erin twenty bucks."

I knit my brows together. This is her reaction? I tell her something as momentous as I've got feelings for one of our besties, and all she can do is tell me she owes Erin money? Then I twig. And yes, I know I was being dense, but in my defense, my mind was still focused on my massive announcement, not on my friends betting on me. "You had a bet with Erin that I would fall for Jason?"

She nods. "Actually, I said you wouldn't. It was Erin who said you would, hence the twenty bucks."

"I can't believe you bet on me. I'm your friend!"

"It was from a long time ago, when you first became roommates."

"*That's* supposed to make me feel better?"

"Does it?"

I shake my head vehemently. "No!"

"Okay. I'm sorry. It was a dumb thing to do."

I harrumph. "You're only saying that because you were wrong."

"But by the looks of you, you'd prefer I was right."

My shoulders slump. "Falling for a guy who's not only my roommate, but a nurse-serial-dater and totally not into me? Yeah, things could be better."

She shoots me a knowing look. "You saw him in just a towel, fresh out of the shower, didn't you?"

I press my lips together and nod.

"I told you that would happen! If you live with a guy long enough, one day you're going to see him in nothing but a towel. How did he look?"

"Good. Great."

"I bet he did." She gets a far off look in her eye.

I snap my fingers. "Darcy? Focus. Massive problem here, remember?"

"Look, we all know Jason's good looking and smart and charming and got that muscular physique of his—"

"Not helping, Darce," I interrupt.

"My point is, you're a woman, he's a man. This was bound to happen, especially after you fell for him when you first met."

"That was a long time ago. Three years! I thought I was on top of those feelings."

"And now you want to get on top of Jason."

I glare at her. "Darcy Evans."

"I'm sorry. Low hanging fruit and all. Look, you got over it before, Soph. You can do it again."

I'm less convinced. "Back then, I didn't know him. It was only lust, you know? Now?" I let out a sigh. "Now—"

"Now he's your friend and your roommate." She shoots me a meaningful look.

"Yup. It'd be too complicated to go there."

"Super complicated. Look, you've had some knocks in the romance department: Andrew, that merman guy."

"The feeder."

"The feeder. How could I forget about him? You're looking for a guy to connect with, and Jason is the logical target. What you've got to do is simply direct that energy somewhere else."

"What do you mean?"

"Find another guy. Not some guy who wants to feed you like you're a baby, not a merman or any other mythical creature. Just a regular, run of the mill, normal guy you think is cute. That way, you're focused on him, not your roommate."

I tap my chin, running the idea through my mind. "You might be onto something."

"Girl, you know I am. Redirect the energies. Find the right guy and it's nothing but a chemical equation."

"Nothing but a chemical equation," I repeat. "Mrs. Forrester would be so proud of us," I reply, naming our high school Chemistry teacher.

"See? You're already making jokes. Bad ones but jokes all the same." Darcy's pretty face creases into a grin. "You've got this."

In an instant, my mind turns to Jason saying those exact words to me over our coffee and cereal.

I blow out a puff of air. "You're right. Redirect the energies, find a chemical equation with another guy. Got it."

As I shoot her an optimistic smile, I ignore the little voice inside telling me it'll never work.

Because it's got to.

Chapter 19

The aroma of a freshly baked cake and piping hot coffee are two of the comforts in life I take great pleasure in. In my job at the Cozy Cottage, I get to indulge myself all day, every day. Today, as the mouth-watering aroma of a freshly baked cake reaches me out by the coffee machine, I feel my tightly-wound shoulders begin to relax, my neck begin to loosen, and my sense of calm slowly begin to return.

Despite my resolve to do as Darcy said and redirect my "energies," those pesky, inconvenient feelings for Jason have been running through my mind all week, grabbing my focus, and twisting me up in knots. It's not a good state of being, and if I could wrinkle my nose and magic these feelings away, I would do it in a heartbeat.

As I froth a large metal pot of steaming hot milk, I chew on my lip. All I've got to do is find a more appropriate subject for my "energies," and everything will return to how it is meant to be.

Easy. Or not . . .

I let out a heavy sigh. Where am I going to find someone who can rival Jason? Mermen, feeders, and the like sure don't make the grade, and with no one else on the horizon, I'll be stuck with being a stammering wreck around Jason from now until eternity.

A voice shakes me out of my self-pity. "Sophie? Earth to Sophie."

I look up to see Paige standing beside me. She's wearing a pretty yellow sundress, a questioning look on her face, her forehead crinkled.

I give myself a mental prod. I can't let my personal life interfere with my job. "Sorry, I was away with the fairies."

"I hope they were fun fairies, but by the looks of you, they weren't."

I shrug, slightly weirded out by the fact I'm discussing imaginary fairies with my boss. "No, just fairies. Nothing to be concerned about."

Her face breaks into a smile. "Good to hear."

"How are you feeling?"

"I have my good days and my not so good days. I'm meeting Bailey out back. Catch you soon?"

"Of course."

As Paige disappears around the door into the kitchen, I refocus my efforts on my day job. What I should be doing is working on my High Tea proposal, not obsessing over my roommate.

I pour the milk into some coffee cups, top the cappuccino off with a dash of powdered chocolate, and deliver them to the customers. Back behind the counter, I remove the coffee machine arm, tap it on the *Grindenstein,* and watch as the used coffee grounds fall out in a disc-like clump.

Bailey comes out of the kitchen and begins to serve the customers as I continue to make their coffee orders. I notice she's a little jumpy, constantly watching the café door. I don't think much of it. Maybe she's expecting her husband, Ryan? It's perfectly understandable for her to feel excited; they are newlyweds after all.

Sometime later, I feel a hand on my arm and look up at Bailey. "Sophie, honey? Can you hold the fort down for a while? I-I need to get something out back."

"Sure."

Her eyes dart toward the café door then she turns back and

shoots me a grin. "Be right back. You stay . . . here," she says before disappearing through the doorway into the kitchen.

I knit my brows together. *Weird.*

With no one waiting to be served, I return my attention to prepping the coffee machine for the mid-morning onslaught. Seriously, I must make hundreds of cups of coffee a day. Strange that I've never counted them before. I wonder how many times I've pulled the arm into place, pressed the button, steamed the milk . . . My thoughts continue down this less than scintillating path until a deep voice says, "Excuse me?"

I drop my cloth on the counter, wipe my hands dry on my polka dot apron, and turn my attention to my new customer. "How can I . . . help . . . you." My words slow as I look up into a set of warm blue eyes behind a pair of glasses, set in a handsome face—a superhero's face. Yup, Clark Kent's doppelgänger is standing in front of me, the cute regular Bailey suggested I ask out way back when we agreed to the No More Bad Dates Pact.

"I'd like one of your fantastic coffees to go, please," Clark Kent says to me as his face creases into a smile.

Even though I know the answer—double shot latte with extra foam—I pretend I don't when I ask, "What would you like?"

"A double shot latte with extra foam, please."

"Coming right up." I grin at him, my belly surprisingly un-butterfly-infested as I gaze at his superhero hotness. Strange. "Do you want a slice of cake with that?"

He leans down to peruse the cakes in the cabinet. There's the apple streusel cake that I personally cannot get enough of, as well as all the other favorites the café is known for. As he straightens up, he pushes his black-rimmed glasses back up his nose. It's totally cute and hot professor-like.

Still no butterflies.

What is wrong with me?

"As tempting as those cakes look, I'm going to have to pass. At the risk of sounding totally lame, I'm in training."

Training for superhero stuff? I don't say it. *Clearly.* But I can't help but think it. Instead, I ask, "For what?"

"Life, I guess."

I feel a smile tease at the edges of my mouth. "You're training for *life?*"

"Sounds, dumb, I know. I used to be a rugby player back in the day, you see. I guess I've always liked to stay in shape. It gets harder as you get older."

My mind instantly brings up an image of the famous All Black Dan Carter, all muscles, pretty face, and nimble footwork. I size him up. He can't be more than late-twenties, thirty tops. "You don't look old."

"I'm positively ancient," he replies with a laugh. "Well, if twenty-nine is considered ancient."

I smile. "It's not. Who did you play for?"

"Well, my university team did pretty well, and then there was the Cyclones. I played for them for a few years until I got onto the New Zealand team."

My eyes spring open wide. "The All Blacks?"

"Yup. A grand total of one game."

I'm seriously impressed with Clark-Kent-slash-Dan-Carter right now. He's a former pro rugby player who represented our country in the mighty All Blacks, and he comes to my café most days of the week? I mean, who knew?

Jason, that's who. Major rugby fan. He'd know exactly who Clark Kent was, and if he were here, he'd be rolling his eyes at me for not recognizing him.

But I'm determined not to think about Jason.

"So, you were seriously good."

He gives a self-effacing shrug. "Good enough, I guess."

"Now I know you're being modest. You played for New Zealand!"

"As I said, only one lousy game."

"What happened?"

"I blew my knee out." A cloud passes briefly over his oh-so pretty face. "Anyway, that's all in the past, and right now, I see an awesome coffee made by a cute girl in my future."

It takes me a full four seconds to tag onto the fact he means me.

Seriously. *I'm* the cute girl. And right on cue, my cheeks begin to heat up. "Oh, I . . . sure. I'll get onto that coffee. Double shot latte with extra foam."

"You've got it." He smiles, and his entire face lights up. He doesn't move from his spot. Instead, he simply stands where he is, watching me.

I glance at him as I slot the coffee arm into place, and he smiles. The guy is totally hot. There's got to be something seriously wrong with me when an ex-All Black who looks like Clark Kent calls me cute and all I manage is one minor blush that I wasn't even particularly committed to.

As I clip the lid onto the takeout cup, Clark Kent slash Dan Carter clears his throat and I turn to look back at him. "Err, I'm not quite sure how to say this, so I'll just come out with it. Your boss? She thought you might be interested in going out with me some time, you know, when your busy coffee-making schedule allows."

My eyebrows spring up to meet my hairline. Did she now? I should be annoyed with Bailey for meddling, especially for not telling me she'd done it. But really, who am I kidding? Rugby-playing Clark Kent might be just what I need to take my mind off certain other people. Maybe I could redirect some of those "energies" to him?

We could create our own chemical equation. *Ugh.* Now I sound like some kind of lame-o song.

When I don't respond, he shifts his weight, looking uncomfortable. "Well, this is awkward. Look, I shouldn't have said anything. I'll just take my coffee to go." He pulls some bills out of his pocket and offers them to me.

I look dumbly down at them. *Snap to it, Sophie!*

"No, really, it's fine."

He does not look convinced. "Fine?"

"More than fine. I-I've been too focused on something else. Sorry."

His handsome face crinkles with confusion. "Ok*aaay*."

"I guess what I'm trying to say is yes, I'm sure I could squeeze a date with you into my busy coffee-making schedule."

Relief visibly washes over him. "That's great. I thought I'd been given a bum steer."

I smile at him, trying to muster the types of feelings I know I should have when a guy as near-perfect as him asks me out. "No bum steer."

"I'm Cameron Lewis, by the way."

"Sophie McCarthy."

"Great to meet you, Sophie."

I tear my eyes from Clark Kent—Cameron—to see Darcy and Erin standing in line behind him. Their eyes are trained eagerly on the two of us, and I shoot them a questioning look.

Cameron turns to them and says, "Sorry, ladies, I'm holding you up." Still with the cash in his outstretched hand, he says, "Thanks for the coffee."

I wave his cash away. "It's on the house, Cameron."

"Thanks, that's really sweet of you." He slides his cash back into his back pocket and then leans across the counter.

I shoot Darcy and Erin a quick look before I lean in to him. I hear Erin say, "Have you seen this lovely painting of a garden over here, Darcy?"

"Please, show me," Darcy replies, about as obvious as the sky is blue, and they wander away from us.

"Well, Sophie, it's been great finally meeting you. And thanks for this." He raises his cup. "I'll drink it and think of you."

"Okay. I'll, ah, give you my number, if you want?"

"That would be great." He pulls out his phone and hands it to me to type my details in.

Out of the corner of my eye, I catch Darcy and Erin with smirks on their faces. So much for looking at that painting.

"Thanks, Sophie. I'll call you," Cameron says.

"I'll look forward to it." I watch him leave, wishing I could feel more. More . . . something. Anything.

I give myself a mental shake-up. He's gorgeous, he's sweet, and he was an All Black, for goodness' sake. What's more, he's interested in me—and he's asked me out.

Why am I not dancing around the room like an ecstatic lunatic?

Isn't this exactly what I've been looking for?

"OMG! Did that totally cute guy just ask you out on a date?" Erin looks all innocent as she and Darcy return to the counter, their faces bright.

"He's a total hottie, Soph. If he did ask you out you should go out with him," Darcy adds.

"Definitely. He's a total smokehouse," Erin confirms.

I narrow my eyes at them both. "So, you two just happened to turn up here to see it all go down, did you?"

"Yes," Erin says.

"Absolutely." This from Darcy.

"Bailey didn't say anything to either of you?"

"Bailey? No," Darcy replies.

I put my hands on my hips. "Come on, you two: confess."

My friends have the good grace to look as sheepish as a couple of ewes in a paddock.

"Bailey might have said something about this cute guy who comes in here at this time most days," Erin replies.

"And we might have suggested she have a word with him and then vacate stage right," Darcy adds. "We thought we'd swing by to check things out."

I try to wrap my mind around what just happened. "Everyone was in on it? Even Paige?"

Erin shakes her head. "She's a little preoccupied right now. You know, baby stuff."

"Plus, her horse lost the race, remember?" Darcy adds. "Oliver the feeder. Crashed and burned."

I harrumph. "More like crash-landed in a bowl of mushy soup, which he then wanted to spoon-feed to me."

Erin giggles. "Now, there's an image. So, you and the smokehouse exchanged numbers, huh?"

"He took mine, so I guess I'll know if he's keen if I hear from him."

Erin gives a sage nod. "Oh, he was keen."

"One hundred percent keen." Darcy's voice is firm, uncompromising when she adds, "He's a good choice, Soph. A *really good choice.*" Although her lips are moving, her eyes are doing the talking. I know what she's telling me: *choose Cameron, not Jason. Cameron's available and interested in you.*

Jason? Well, that would be a hard no on both counts.

"A good choice? Are you kidding?" Erin is incredulous. "He's gorgeous! Sophie is so lucky."

"You know he's a former rugby player, Erin?" I say.

She looks surprised. "He is?"

"Yup. Played for the Cyclones and one game for the All Blacks. And you don't like jocks, remember?"

"Well, *I'm* not the one dating him," she replies smugly. "Come on, Soph. He's perfect."

"You're right," I say with a brisk nod. "He's perfect and I'm really lucky he's asked me out."

"Atta girl," Darcy says.

"Right. Coffee?" I offer.

As I go about making my friends their coffees, I harden my resolve. Cameron Lewis is just the guy to take my mind off Jason.

And I'm determined to make it work.

Chapter 20

I spend the next few days focusing on two things: working on my High Tea proposal and avoiding Jason like the Bubonic Plague. Although the first thing should be my absolute key priority, it's virtually impossible to keep Jason from seeping into my consciousness, like a spilled glass of red wine into carpet.

Yup, much like Lady Macbeth in Shakespeare's famous play, Jason has become a "damned spot" I simply cannot get out. (Although, unlike in *Macbeth*, I don't have the invisible blood of King Duncan on my hands, and I'm sincerely hoping I don't go mad in the process.)

Sean would be so proud of me.

"Hey, Sophie. What are you doing here?"

I look up from scribbling notes in my notepad and blink at the guy standing by my table. "Oliver." I try to inject some enthusiasm into my voice, but really, Oliver "feeder" Price is the last person I want to see, particularly when I have a cake stand stacked with delectable treats currently placed on the table in front of me. Let's face it, that's akin to having a line of tequila shots in front of an alcoholic.

I paste on a smile. "I'm, ah, doing some research."

"For the high tea place you work at?"

I nod. "Cozy Cottage High Tea."

He taps the side of his nose. "I won't tell anyone."

What would it matter if he did? "Err, thanks?"

He looks around the room. "This place is awesome, isn't it?"

I glance at the lavish surrounds of Operatic, a high tea spot in the affluent suburb of Newmarket in central Auckland. Like the other handful of high tea places I've visited in the last couple of weeks—the diet to fit back into my pants begins tomorrow—it's got the ubiquitous chandeliers, crisp white tablecloths, and quiet and refined atmosphere. No one seems to talk above a whisper, and everyone seems to be on their very best behavior.

It's all a little yawn-worthy.

"I love their little eclairs, and their mini smoked trout sandwiches, and those tiny scones with jam and cream," Oliver says with enthusiasm.

Is there any food he doesn't like? "You're right. They're all so good."

"What I like about them the most, though, is that you can eat them whole. No need to even bite off a chunk."

I push an image away of Oliver stuffing morsel after morsel into my mouth until it's totally full of mini sandwiches and little eclairs. "Yes, bite-size is very . . . convenient."

Just as I'm hoping this conversation is done, a pretty woman about my age in a bright pink dress approaches us and smiles at me. "Hi," she says as she takes Oliver's hand in hers.

He plants a kiss on her cheek, turns to me, and says, "This is Cleo. We're on a date."

My eyebrows ping upwards. Oh, that poor girl. She has no idea what she's in for. "Hi, Cleo. I'm Sophie. Is this your first date?"

"Oh, no. I think this is our ninth."

"It's our tenth, pumpkin," Oliver corrects.

Ten dates? *Huh.* Maybe he hasn't tried his spoon-feeding trick on her yet?

"Is it? How could I have forgotten one of our dates?"

Oliver wraps his arm around her shoulders. "It's no big deal, honey."

She pushes her bottom lip out and replies, "It is to me." Thankfully, the pouting lasts for a limited time—pouting women is right up at the top of my pet peeves list—before she looks back at me. "How do you two know each other, then?" She lifts her tone from petulant child to actual adult.

"Oh, through a friend a while back," I say.

Oliver puts his hands up in the air. "Okay, full disclosure, snicker doodle: Sophie and I dated."

I'm almost too sidetracked by the "snicker doodle" nickname to respond. "Oh, it was just one date, really, and it was over before it began," I explain hastily.

"I don't mind," Cleo says to me with a shake of her pretty head. She turns her gaze to Oliver. "We all have our pasts, don't we, baby cakes?"

Oliver cups her face in his hand and gazes at her. "You're such a wonderful person. Do you know that, pudding?"

Baby cakes? Pudding? Added to a list that includes snicker doodle as a term of endearment and I'm beginning to feel pretty darn queasy.

After a moment of mutual gazing, they seem to realize I'm still sitting here beside them like the dumb third wheel I am.

"It was great to see you, Sophie."

"Yes. You, too, Oliver," I lie.

He spies something on my cake stand, and his eyes light up. "Ooh, we didn't try a lime and avocado mini cheesecake." He looks at me, and I know exactly what he's going to ask before the words spill out. "Would it be weird if we tried one?"

I want to scream out that this whole thing is weird, but instead, I simply nod. What else am I going to do? He scoops one of the cheesecakes up, takes a bite, then pops the rest into "babycake's" open mouth.

"Mmm. So good," Cleo replies with a big grin.

Cleo likes the spoon-feeding. I guess Oliver's found his perfect mate.

"Come on, sugar-daddy, take me home," she coos.

Sugar-daddy? Oh, I'm definitely queasy now.

Thankfully, they say their goodbyes, and I'm left to contemplate whether I can stomach eating anything after their little display.

Oliver has a girlfriend, a fully grown woman who clearly enjoys being fed. I guess what weirds one person out makes another person happy. And they did look happy together. I guess it just goes to show, there's someone out there for everyone.

It's not that I'm *not* happy for Oliver. Far from it. In fact, I'm ecstatically happy for him. It's just . . . I guess I want what he has with Cleo—well, not with Cleo exactly, and definitely not that whole weird feeding thing they're into. Gross. No, what I want is to find someone who makes me smile. Someone I feel totally at ease with. Someone who gets me. Someone who gets my pulse racing and makes my belly flip and flop all over the place whenever I think of him.

Maybe someone who looks amazing fresh out of the shower in nothing but a towel . . .?

Argh! No, no, no, no, no!

I cannot go there. It's not Jason. It can't be. He's wrong for me on so many levels. Layers and layers of levels stacked high into the clouds like a freaking skyscraper.

Levels like the fact we're roommates, and messing that up would make home life beyond awkward.

Levels like he's a serial cute-and-perky-nurse-dater, with a revolving door policy on relationships.

Levels like we're friends, *best* friends, and everyone knows friends and romance don't mix.

Don't they?

Seriously, there is no planet in this solar system where Jason and I can be together.

Deep in the layers of my skyscraper visualization, I must look like I'm in some sort of haze because one of the servers asks me if I'm okay, his features creased in concern. "Is there something you're unhappy with, miss?" he asks as he gestures at the virtually untouched food on the three-tiered cake stand on my table.

"Absolutely not. It all looks delicious." And just to prove that I'm a perfectly normal person who isn't obsessing about her roommate, I pluck a slice of smoked salmon atop a pumpernickel round from the stand and pop it in my mouth.

And it *is* delicious. All of it. Despite wanting to, I cannot fault the food in this place, or in any of the places I've visited.

Which makes my task of pulling a proposal on how to resurrect High Tea's flailing customer numbers so much harder.

I'M SPRAWLED out on the sofa, my belly full of the Operatic treats I indulged in earlier in the day, when I get a text from Cameron, asking me to go out with him the next day.

Are you free for drinks tomorrow night?

Of course I can't meet him tomorrow night. Rules of the No More Bad Dates Pact clearly state Initial Contact must be over coffee during the day. No liquor to influence decision making, cold light of day rational thinking required.

I tap out my reply.

Can we meet for coffee in the morning tomorrow instead? You name the place.

My phone pings straight away with his reply, naming a café I've not been to before in the central city. I picture Cameron in all his tall, athletic, Clark Kent glory. If anyone can help me conquer my feelings for Jason, Superman can.

He's got to.

I hear the key in the lock and sit bolt upright. My nerves instantly zing around inside at the prospect of seeing the one person I've been working hard at avoiding.

Oblivious to my internal turmoil, Jason breezes into the living room in a pair of shorts and a T-shirt that's tight enough around his upper arms to show off his muscles, and slim-fitting enough to do more than hint at the buff torso beneath. And yes, I know what you're thinking. Why did I look? If I'm working so hard at avoiding him, why let myself down by gawping at him now? It's a very good question.

All I can say is Superman, I need you now . . .

Jason's face breaks into a grin when he sees me. "Hey, McCarthy. How's it going?" He wanders over to the kitchen and pulls a bottle of water out of the refrigerator, pops the cap, and takes a long drink.

"It's going great, thanks. Just great." I clear my throat and avert my gaze. Finally. Instead, I choose to concentrate on a scatter cushion on the sofa next to me. It's one Mom gave me for my birthday a couple of years back. It's got an image of a Parisian cat in a beret, a cup of coffee in hand—or should that be "in paw?"—as it looks out at me with a self-assured grin. "I bet you don't have to deal with inappropriate crushes on your roommate," I mutter under my breath to the cat.

Yup, things have gotten that bad, people.

I hear footsteps and look up to see Jason leave the room. I sigh. "Oh, to be a French cat with nothing to worry about than the fact you don't have opposing thumbs to hold your cup of coffee."

The cat doesn't reply.

"I bet your name is Gerard or Pierre or something like that."

No response.

"Oh, I know, you're François the French Feline."

The sound of Jason's water bottle against the glass coffee table pulls me out of my mildly insane feline ponderings. He flops down onto the sofa next to me. "Who the heck are you talking to, McCarthy?"

"No one." Embarrassed, I push the French cat cushion behind my back and shift over to get as far away from him as I can. "I assume you've been to the gym?"

He arcs an eyebrow. "Do I smell that bad?"

I don't dare risk inhaling his scent for fear of what it may do to me, so I fan my nose and say, "It's pretty bad."

"Oh, well. I guess a man has got to get a bit stinky in the process." He flexes his arm muscle, and says, "This doesn't just happen by itself, you know. It's long, hard workouts and tireless dedication."

I let out a jittery laugh as I drag my gaze from his bulging bicep. Where's that French cat when I need him? Oh, yeah, I'm currently squashing him against the back of the sofa.

Thankfully, Jason relaxes his arm and leans back. "How was your day? Weren't you doing more research or something?"

"I went to Operatic." I pat my belly. "I'm so full, I can barely move."

"It was good, huh?"

"Yeah, it was. All the places I've visited have been amazing. Great food, gorgeous interiors, everything is elegant and refined. And they're busy, like all the time. I'm really struggling to work out how to fix High Tea."

"You'll come up with something. I know you will."

Because he has faith in me.

Thoughts like this are not helping me kick my Jason obsession. I've got to focus on something I don't like about him. Something like the fact he sometimes makes the coffee too strong in the morning, or the fact he leaves his towel draped across the bath sometimes instead of hanging it on the rail.

I can hear a voice in the back of my head asking, "Is that all you got?" I slump my shoulders in defeat.

Yeah, I got nothing.

"You okay, Soph?"

I come back to reality to see Jason peering at me, his handsome face creased with mildly amused concern.

"Oh, of course. Sorry. I was in la-la land."

Thinking about you.

"Thinking about High Tea?"

"Yes, absolutely. That's what I was doing; thinking about High Tea."

Not what it would feel like to have those strong, muscular arms wrapped around me as we're locked in a passionate, toe-curling, utterly breathtaking kiss.

Definitely not that.

"Here's what I think. You've got a great place with delicious food, all served up in those ridiculously small sizes."

"Bite-size."

"More like chick-sized. Give me a man-sized burger any day."

"I thought you were going to tell me what you thought about how to fix High Tea?"

His eyes dance when he replies, "I can share my love of burgers too, can't I?"

I let out a light laugh as the extreme awkwardness I was feeling only moments ago begins to diminish.

"Anyway, my point is, all these places have similar offerings, right? So far, so universal. What I would do if I were you would be to look at what Cozy Cottage High Tea either does or can start to do that's different."

I nod as his idea sinks in, "It's U.S.P."

"U.S.P.?"

I prop my elbow up on the sofa arm. "Are you telling me I know something *Doctor* Christie doesn't know?" I tease.

"I would hope you know a whole load of stuff I don't know, for your sake. Otherwise, you're in way deeper trouble than I thought."

I grin at him. "Oh, I know plenty."

This. This is what I want. Talking, teasing one another, everything between us relaxed and easy going. The old Jason and Sophie. Roommates. Friends.

Not all twisted up in knots over wanting him when I know I shouldn't. Time to move on dot com. #GetOverIt.

"In case you want to know, U.S.P. stands for Unique Selling Point. It's what Cozy Cottage High Tea has that other high tea places do not."

"Exactly. Find the 'U.S.P.,'" he uses air quotes, "and you've got the magic formula."

I tap my chin in the internationally recognized "I'm thinking" gesture. And then it hits me, right like that, right out of the blue. I know what the Cozy Cottage has got that the other places haven't. I know its U.S.P.

My pulse speeds up and I feel a lightness in my chest. I look up at Jason. "I think I just cracked it."

"That was fast, even for a mastermind ninja like you."

"Think about it. Who knows the Cozy Cottage better than me?"

"Its owners?"

"Well, sure, but they haven't been able to make High Tea work. And I think I might have a hunch why."

"Why?"

I bite my lip. "I need to get my head straight first. But I think this is going to be great!"

His smile is full of warmth when he says, "You're so cute when you're excited."

Despite all my efforts to deny the way I feel, my heart swells. Suddenly, I'm all awkward around him once more. "I'll, ah, go work on that idea now." I hop up from the sofa.

"Right, I'd better go get showered and dressed. I'm out for dinner tonight."

"With Megan?" I ask and am embarrassed when my voice comes out all breathy.

"Actually, yes."

I try not to let it sting. "That's got to be a record for you. All the other nurses in the line must be getting annoyed by now," I joke.

He stands up beside me, and I work hard at not noticing how tall and imposing he is. Tall, imposing, and completely gorgeous.

Dear Lord, help me.

"There's no line, McCarthy, just a seemingly endless pool of willing participants."

I roll my eyes. "You're impossible, you know that?"

He gives a shrug before he collects his empty water bottle from the table. "I'm just giving the people what they want. And tonight, that's dinner at Chez Pierre."

I swallow, my chest tightening. "You're going to Chez Pierre?

"Yeah. I'll have to resist the urge to try to feed anyone while I'm there, though."

"Oh, very freaking funny. Actually, I've got a date myself

coming up soon." I watch his face for a reaction and am secretly pleased when I detect what might just be a hint of concern.

"You mean an Initial Contact, and then we'll need to interrogate him until we break him."

"You won't break him. I bet he'll pass with flying colors. He's really sweet, and a really great guy." Yup, I'm laying it on thick here.

He shakes his head. "That's how it all begins. Even the merman looked good to you in the beginning, remember? Before you found out he likes to swim around in people's pools with his perfectly serviceable legs jammed into a fake fish fin."

Channeling the nonchalant attitude of François the French cat, I wave his acerbic comment away with a flick of the wrist. "Cameron's nothing like him. He used to play rugby, and he's in great shape."

"McCarthy, a lot of guys played rugby."

"For New Zealand?"

His mouth forms an "o." "He played for New Zealand?"

I press my lips together, enjoying his reaction. "That's right. Although the poor guy got injured and had to retire. He still looks like he could be a professional sportsman, though. In fact, Cameron looks like Dan Carter crossed with Superman."

"Cameron?"

I nod. "Cameron Lewis. Why? Do you know who he is?"

Jason's jaw is on the floor. As suspected, he knows precisely who he is. "Ah, yeah, I do. He was the best halfback the Cyclones had in years. His career was over after one lousy game for the All Blacks. He shattered the country's dream."

I use air quotes when I reply, "'Shattering the country's dream' seems a little over the top, Jas, even for a mad rugby fan like you."

He wanders to the kitchen to collect his phone from the counter and types something in. He turns the phone around, and I see an image of Cameron dressed in a Cyclones team uniform. The camera has caught him as he's running, ball tucked under one arm, his leg muscles strong and pronounced. His brows are knitted together in concentration and he looks every bit the strong, manly rugby player he is.

I take the phone from Jason and study the image. "That's him. I didn't recognize him when we were talking, but now that I see him dressed like this, I know I've seen him play on TV."

"You have. With me, right here in our apartment."

I concentrate on the image. "Cameron Lewis, huh? All those rugby games I sat through with you, and now I'm going on a date with a star player."

Jason's mouth twists, and I think I detect something lurking beneath the surface. "It sucked when he got injured. The All Blacks needed him. His country needed him. The man had such potential."

I hand him back his phone. "Well, I would have to agree with that statement."

I'm not proud. I know I'm teasing him. I thought it would make me feel better. I thought it might help to push my feelings for Jason away. It doesn't. It only makes me want him all the more. Especially when I see the look on his face. If I didn't know better, I'd say he looks . . . hurt.

What the flipping heck am I doing?

He pulls his lips together into a line. "Well, I hope he's what you're looking for, Soph. I'll, ah, catch you later, I guess." He drops his empty water bottle into the recycling bin and walks down the hallway. A moment later, I hear his door close.

Great work, Sophie! I've teased the guy I want to be with over a guy I don't want to be with, and now he's clearly unhappy with me.

I wander back to the sofa, flop down, and balance the cat cushion on my knees. François the French Feline is slightly creased from being shoved into the back of the sofa but otherwise fine. I smooth the cushion out with my hand. At the risk of sounding like I've completely lost my grip on reality, I whisper, "François, what am I going to do?"

François, arrogant French cat that he is, does not respond.

Chapter 21

I sit at a small table at Jimmy's Café and wait, feeling about as comfortable and at home as a Kardashian in a library. Although I've walked past Jimmy's on my way to the Cozy Cottage more times than I can remember, I've never been inside. I look at all the black and white photos of who I can only assume is Jimmy himself, with various B, C, and D local celebrities adorning the walls.

I'm here for my Initial Contact with Cameron. It's not that he's late. I got here early, hoping I'd have time to compose myself before he got here—by which I mean get Jason out of my head so I can concentrate on the guy I'm supposed to be interested in. The guy who's actually interested in me.

I don't have to wait long. I spot Cameron as he steps into the café and scans the room. I raise my hand to give a small wave and am rewarded with a beaming smile that tells me he's happy to see me.

In a few short strides, he's by my table. "Hi, Sophie. You look beautiful."

I feel heat rise in my cheeks as I stand to give him a quick hug. "You look good, too. I'm glad we're doing this." I sit back down, and he takes the seat opposite me.

"I've wanted to talk to you for ages."

"You have?"

He nods. "You know, I work about a fifteen-minute drive from the Cozy Cottage Café, but I go there several times a week for my coffee."

"We do good coffee."

He gives me a smile. "That's true, but there's another reason. I kinda like the barista."

I blink at him in disbelief. "You drive fifteen minutes for your daily fix so you can see me?"

"Crazy, right?"

"No, not at all," I gush. "It's sweet and romantic and, well, it's not something I thought anyone would do for me."

He crinkles his forehead. "Why not?"

I shrug. "I don't know. I'm just a regular girl."

"Well, you're a regular girl I've wanted to get to know for a while now."

I lift my eyes to the heavens. *Seriously?* You're offering me a hot guy who's so totally into me he goes to great lengths to see me now? *Now?* Where was Cameron before Oliver, before Mr. Merman?

Before my feelings changed for Jason?

He pulls a face. "I sound like a stalker, don't I?"

I look up into his gorgeous blue eyes, set in his handsome super-hero face. "God, no! You sound . . . perfect."

"Perfect?" He laughs. "I've been called many things in my life, but one thing I've not been called is perfect."

"What are some of the things you've been called?"

"Let's see. There was 'Cam the Man' for a time in high school when I was on the rugby team. That's one of my personal favorites."

"For obvious reasons."

"Then there was my nickname when I was at the Cyclones: Tarzan."

"Let me guess. Was it because you had long hair and ran around the jungle in a loincloth talking to the animals?" I tease.

His laugh is low and rumbles through me. "How did you know?

I think it was more to do with the hair. I used to wear it longer when I was young. Oh, there was this other one I got from a girlfriend. She used to call me Superman. Can you believe it?"

I clear my throat. "Really? Superman, huh? How weird."

"I know, right? I think it's because of the glasses. They give me a Clark Kent vibe, she used to say."

I narrow my eyes at him. "Yeah, I guess I can see that."

"How about you? Any nicknames?"

My mind instantly darts to "McCarthy," the name Jason calls me. "My last name doesn't count, right?"

He shakes his head. "Nope."

"Okay. Well, my older brother used to call me 'baby.'"

"When you were an actual baby?"

"Right up to when I was, I don't know, twenty-five?"

He laughs once more. "Are you twenty-five right now?"

"I am. But seriously, he hasn't called me that for days," I reply with a grin.

We continue our light and flirty banter over coffee until we reach the business end of the date: the part when I've got to tell him about the next step in the No More Bad Dates Pact Vetting Process.

Despite the absence of butterflies or belly flips, I want this to work with Cameron. Maybe those butterflies are late? Maybe they'll arrive with reinforcements shortly and I'll barely be able to look at him without swooning?

"Hold up. You're telling me that this isn't a first date, that it's in fact . . . a what did you call it?"

"An Initial Meeting. I know, it sounds crazy, but we figured we need to see if we have a rapport with the guy before we put him through the next step."

"This doesn't sound good."

"No, it's fine. Really. All you've got to do is meet my friends before we go on our first official date. If you want to, I mean," I add hurriedly.

"Just meet your friends? No tying me to a chair and shining a bright light in my eyes as you drip water onto my forehead?"

I laugh. "We could do that if you wanted. Usually, it's just having a chat over a drink. They'll ask you some questions about honesty and conflict. That kind of thing."

His eyes are soft when he says, "Being vetted by your friends doesn't sound too grisly. I have a feeling you're worth it, Sophie McCarthy. Just name the place and I'll be there."

"Is Jojo's Karaoke Bar this Saturday night at seven okay with you?"

"I love that place! I'm not the best singer in the world, but karaoke is totally fun. I've been a few times with a bunch of friends."

I beam at him. Superman loves karaoke. Who knew?

With our Initial Contact done and dusted, I say goodbye to Cameron and begin my walk down the street for a meeting with my two bosses at the Cozy Cottage. Today's the day I'm presenting my ideas for High Tea, and I feel certain I've found the missing piece in the formula that will lift those all-important customer numbers.

With every step I take, I feel more and more positive about Cameron. Maybe Darcy is totally right? All I needed was another target for those attraction energies to hone in on. Cameron Lewis, with his good looks and gentle charm, is the perfect choice. I pick up my pace at the prospect, almost breaking into a skip.

I'm Colin Firth as Mr. Darcy in that nineties version of *Pride and Prejudice*: I *can* conquer this. I can. Like Mr. Darcy does for Elizabeth Bennett, I can beat my feelings for Jason, and come out the other side, ready to fall for Cameron.

I slow my gait as my mind races to the finish line. Mr. Darcy doesn't beat his feelings for Lizzie. He tries and he fails. In fact, he falls helplessly and completely in love with her, then marries her in a pretty cheesy double wedding with Lizzie's sister and his best buddy, and they live happily ever after.

Together.

Okay, bad analogy.

I slump my shoulders and come to a complete stop in the middle of the sidewalk. Some old guy grumbles about inconsiderate youth as he narrowly misses me, but I'm barely paying any attention.

I wrack my brain for another famous example and come up with *nada*. I'm not deterred. Even though I can't think of a single example, I know I'm like . . . someone else who conquered their feelings and moved on. That's what I'm like. Someone who killed the feelings off like bad guys in a video game, well and truly blew them into smithereens. That's me, the conquering blower upper of feelings, who successfully redirected them to the right guy, and lived to tell the tale, triumphant and free!

Only, I've got no freaking idea how I'm ever going to do it.

———

I STAND in the empty High Tea as Bailey and Paige look up at me in expectation. It's a quiet time of the day and Alex is "manning" the café, as he chose to put it. I've got my laptop hooked up to an overhead projector, which is currently beaming the title of my presentation onto the plain white wall.

"First up, thank you both for trusting me to come up with a proposal for High Tea. You both know how much this place means to me, and I really want to help you make it a major success."

"We're excited to see what you've come up with, Sophie. Aren't we, Bailey?" Paige says.

Bailey nods. "Oh, absolutely."

There's a note in her voice that pricks my ears up. Bailey's usually so enthusiastic and positive, and right now her words don't reflect her tone.

I push it from my mind. I'm hoping the solution I've come up with will mean we can get High Tea back on track—and I can keep my Weekend Manager's job.

I click my mouse to change the slide. I point at the figures beamed onto the wall. "I did a profit and loss to show you where things are at right now. Customer numbers are down on this time last year, our costs are static, but our profits are in decline." I study my bosses' faces. Their mouths form thin lines as they study the wall. "It's grim reading, but we need to see where we're starting from so we can get a baseline. Compare that to the café." I click my mouse again, and a fresh set of much more impressive numbers are beamed onto the wall. "You can see that High Tea is being carried by its much more profitable neighbor."

"You're great with numbers, Sophie. That all makes sense to me," Paige says.

"It might make sense, but it's not pretty reading," Bailey comments.

"I know it doesn't look good for High Tea, but I have an idea." I click on my mouse once more and up pops a new image with a big red heart, front and center. "As you know, I've been doing some research. The customers I spoke to here said they loved High Tea. Always nice to hear, but so far, so *not* useful." I shoot them a rueful smile as I click to the next slide. "Then, I visited a bunch of high tea places around the city. All of them had delicious food at a similar price point to us, they were all open every day, and every single one of them had fancy, classy surrounds, like in the image." I point at the photo of Operatic, with its chandeliers, soft chairs, and romantic interior. "Yes, they look luxurious and inviting, and yes they look higher-end than Cozy Cottage High Tea. That's part of their appeal, and where we're falling short. The people I spoke to said they see going out for high tea as an indulgence, whereas I think we market it as an extension of the café experience."

"I hope you're going somewhere with this because right now, I'm feeling pretty depressed," Bailey says.

"Next image," I reply with a smile. I click on the mouse to show an image of Operatic with a big red cross. "Every single one of those places was super quiet and refined. People talked in hushed voices, and the servers were all very calm and polite. Now, I'm not suggesting we get rude servers. What I am suggesting is we bring some more of the fun from the café into High Tea."

Paige knits her brows together. "Maybe I'm being dense or maybe I've got pregnancy brain, if that's really a thing, but I'm not following you."

"Let me back up, then. What do people love about the Cozy Cottage? It's the warmth, the feeling of being in the comfort of home, only with much better food and coffee. We offer them that in a casual, relaxed atmosphere in the café."

"That's the thing that brought me here as a customer, before I worked here," Paige adds.

"Exactly. Then there's our Friday Night Jam, which is super popular for a very good reason: people love to get together for a drink and a bite to eat with their friends and listen to some good music." I move to the next image. It's of the Friday Night Jam. "What I'm suggesting is we bring music and that special Cozy Cottage atmosphere to High Tea, only make it fancier, so people know it's a treat."

"Music? We haven't thought of that," Bailey says.

"That's because no other high tea place does it other than soft, background muzac. We can get local performers, like we do for the Jams, and extend the liquor license to serve drinks in here. That's the other thing the high tea places do that we don't: liquor."

"You're telling us we need to be less like our competition? Oh, I like that idea," Paige says.

"Yes! That's exactly what I'm saying. We need to capitalize on our U.S.P.: our warmth, our sense of fun. That's how I see us turning High Tea's profits around." I hold my breath, my hands clenched at my sides as I await their verdict.

They share a look I can't quite see before Bailey turns back to me and says, "You sure have given us something to think about, Sophie."

"Well, I love it," Paige announces. "Totally love it. Cozy Cottage is our heart and our soul. The way you suggest bringing more of it in here is so darn logical! What made you think of music?"

"Someone pointed out to me that the Cozy Cottage has something special," I reply.

"Well, whoever that someone is, you need to kiss them because this is fantastic," Paige says.

I press my lips together and do my best to ignore the way the butterflies in my belly start a dance party at the prospect of kissing Jason. A slow, sexy, tender kiss as he runs his fingers up my neck and buries them deep in my hair . . .

Okay, so expelling Jason from my consciousness is clearly a work in progress. But I *am* working on it.

Paige pushes herself up from her chair. "Thanks, Sophie. We're going to talk about this, aren't we, Bailey? But right now, I've got to pee. Again. I love these babies, really I do, but they take up so much room!"

My relief comes out as a laugh as Paige waddles past me and gives me a pat on the arm. "Good work, Sophie."

As I close my laptop and flick the lights on, Bailey says, "It seems so obvious now that you've presented it to us. Why did we not 'Cozy Cottage' the crap out of this place before? All we did was use the same décor and serve some of the same food. We could have done so much more."

I lift my shoulders in a shrug. "Sometimes we can't see things that are staring us in the face."

"I guess not. Sophie, thank you so much for going to this extra effort for us. You are amazing, and we're so lucky to have you."

Warmth spreads across my chest at Bailey's compliment. "I've got a selfish reason for doing it, too. I want to keep my Weekend Manager's role."

Bailey's smile is tense, and I wonder whether my proposal is too little and too late. "Paige and I will talk about it and come back to you."

As I unhook the projector from my laptop, a seed of doubt begins to grow inside me, and my belly forms a tight knot. The numbers show a bleak truth, and right now, my ideas are only that: ideas.

Could it be that it's already too late to save High Tea?

Chapter 22

The evening of Cameron's Vetting Process rolls around after a busy work week, and I've got so many mixed emotions about tonight, they could stick a decorative umbrella in my head and make me a new cocktail. "The Sophie" is a mixture of nerves, denial, fear, and excitement, with a healthy dose of misplaced feelings for the wrong guy I'm hoping I can redirect.

"You look super cute tonight, Soph," Darcy says to me as we place our drinks on our usual table at Jojo's and take our seats. "That red dress has got total x-factor."

Self-conscious, I smooth my slim-fitting dress down. "You think?"

"Total va va voom, you mean," Erin says.

"Yes, if this were the nineteen-forties, Erin," Darcy replies with a chortle.

"Sophie looks this good because she's going on a date with a certain super-hot former pro rugby player." Erin grins at me. "After he's passed the Vetting Process, of course. But then he is Superman. No problem for him. Tall buildings in a single bound and all that."

"I'm sure *Cameron* will love the dress," Darcy says, her eyes trained on me.

I know exactly what she's getting at. As part of the No More Bad Dates Pact Committee, Jason is due to arrive any minute for Cameron's vetting. When I put the dress on tonight, I told myself it was for Cameron alone. But I'd be a cold-faced liar if I didn't admit to the hope that Jason might see me in it and . . . and what? Decide I'm the woman for him? Leave Megan for me?

I'm deluding myself, and Jason and Megan appear to be a "thing." That's right, Jason Christie, slayer of nurses, serial short-term dater extraordinaire, appears to have a proper, bona fide girlfriend.

And I'm happy about it. Really, I am. *Super* happy. With Jason all cozily loved-up with Megan, visiting romantic spots like Chez Pierre together, I know there is zero chance my feelings for him will be reciprocated. That means I can let those annoying feelings die a natural death—or bludgeon them violently with a hammer. You know, whichever works.

And in the meantime, I can focus entirely on Cameron.

"Oh, my gosh. Look. He's here," Erin says.

I look up, fully expecting to see Jason. Instead, I spot Cameron. I clench my jaw as I work to ignore the sinking feeling in my belly.

Cameron sees me and gives a brief wave before he strides over to our table.

"He's even more of a total smokehouse than I remember," Erin says.

"So, you only dislike current pro sportsmen, not former ones?" Darcy teases her.

"I'm making an exception, okay?" Erin replies under her breath.

"Hello, ladies." Cameron's smile is warm as his eyes land on me. "Wow, Sophie. You look incredible in that dress."

I stand and take his extended hand in mine. Erin's right, he is a total smokehouse, with his good looks and confident demeanor.

"Hey, Cameron," I say.

He leans in and kisses me on the cheek. "I, ah, don't know what the protocol is with this pact of yours, so I hope this is okay."

"Oh, of course it is," I reply hurriedly. "Do you have a drink? There's no table service here so you'll need to get it from the bar."

"Right. Okay. I'll go get a drink. Anyone else need a fresh one?"

"We're good, but thank you *so* much for offering, Cameron." Erin is gazing at him like a love-struck teen. I nudge her under the table, and she drags her eyes away from him, mouthing, "What?"

"Okay. Back in a few."

With Cameron on his way to the bar, Erin lets out a sigh. "You are so freaking lucky, girl. He is a beautiful, beautiful man."

Darcy laughs. "I think you're laying it on a bit thick there, honey. And anyway, he's here for Sophie."

I watch Cameron. He's leaning his elbow on the bar as he places his order with the barman, and I get a fine view of his athletic physique. Really, he's any woman's ideal guy. I'd be a total fool to let him slip through my fingers because I'm hung up on my roommate.

"Where's Jas? I thought he was coming tonight," Erin asks.

"He said he'd be here," Darcy replies. "He's a rugby nut so I can't imagine him missing this opportunity to meet a former All Black."

"Oh, I'm sure he'll be here," I say as casually as I can muster.

But he doesn't show, and I find myself scanning the room for him every few minutes. I try to concentrate on Cameron's response when Erin asks him about compromise. I force myself to listen as Darcy asks him about conflict resolution. I even slap my cheeks a couple of times to dislodge myself from Jason's grip on me when Cameron replies to my question about whether he's a romantic.

But really, it's no use. I should never have agreed to this. As perfect as Cameron is in so many ways, it all boils down to one thing: he doesn't have my heart.

I gave that away to a man who didn't even bother to come tonight.

I'm such an idiot.

While Cameron's answering Darcy's question about trust, I excuse myself from the table and make my way to the ladies' room. I lean my hands on the cold sink and stare at my reflection in the dimly-lit room.

What am I doing? There's a great guy out there, putting himself through our stupid No More Bad Dates Vetting Process, willing to answer all the ridiculously probing questions my friends pepper him with, and what do I do? Sit on the edge of my seat, waiting for my no-show roommate.

My shoulders slump as I let out a heavy breath.

I need to move on. I need to shake myself up and get back out there. Cameron's the guy for me. He's here and he's into me.

Two things Jason is not.

When I get back to our table, Cameron and my friends are looking through the list of karaoke songs together.

Cameron looks up as I take my seat, and says, "Are you a duet kinda girl?"

"A what?"

"I'm thinking Sonny and Cher *I Got You Babe*. Not too challenging for a lame singer like myself." He gives me a self-deprecating smile, and I shoot my friends a questioning look.

"He passed," Darcy states simply.

I turn to Cameron. "Hey, that's, err . . . great."

"Apparently, I have 'excellent date potential.' Which is something I can honestly say I have never been told in my entire life."

"So, you get to celebrate your first date with a duet," Erin announces. "We put your names on the list. Cam tells us he's a pretty terrible singer, so we figured you two were a good match."

Cam? They've got all buddy-buddy with him now. How long was I in the ladies' room?

"Are you happy with this level of abuse from your friends?" he asks me with a smile.

"Oh, I'm used to it. And besides, they're totally right."

We spend the next hour or two together singing, laughing, and having fun. Cameron's a great sport, and the girls stick around at my request, even though the meaningful looks Darcy keeps throwing me tells me she's guessed why.

When I announce that I need to go because I've got work in the morning, Cameron walks me out to my car.

"That started out as the weirdest date of my life," he says.

"Intense, huh?"

Standing by my car, he steps closer to me, his eyes trained on mine. "You could say that. But in my opinion, it was totally worth it." He places his hand on my arm and smiles at me.

I know what's coming next. I've been on dates, I know the drill.

My mouth begins to dry out. Although I've enjoyed Cameron's company tonight, and he really is a genuinely great guy, try as I might, I can't seem to drum up the sorts of things I should be feeling for him. Things like wanting to do what he so clearly wants to do with me right now.

I step back, my butt smooching up against my car. "Well, that's just super. Thanks for, ah, that."

His eyes are electric as he steps even closer to me.

My mouth is now about as dry as summer in the no-rain city of Lima as I fumble around for the door handle behind me.

"Sophie."

"What? Yes? Oh."

He circles his hands around my waist and stops my words with his lips. And it's a good kiss. Great, even. Soft but confident, long enough to show me he means business, not too long that it's all a bit too much. Really, I can't fault his technique.

It's just . . . he's not Jason.

"Do you have any clue how long I've wanted to do that?" he asks as he pulls away.

"Ah, no," I murmur. My insides twist into a painful knot.

"Let's just say I don't drink nearly as much Cozy Cottage coffee as I buy."

I know I've got to say something to him. Put him out of his misery. Under any other circumstances, I'd be in seventh heaven to date someone like him.

It's time to come clean.

I study my hands. "I'm sorry, Cameron. I-I can't do this."

"Do what?"

When I don't answer, he gently cups my chin in his hand, and I look up into his eyes. "I can't go out with you. And I'm so, so sorry to have put you through all that vetting stuff. It's just—"

He raises his eyebrows as he waits for my explanation. "It's just what?"

I let out a heavy sigh as my chest tightens at the thought of Jason. I've been so busy fighting the way I feel about him, it's only now, with Cameron looking so intently into my eyes, that I can finally admit what I feel to myself.

I hang my head as a sense of complete and utter hopelessness washes over me. "I'm in love with someone else."

Because that's what this is. Love.

I know it as well as I know myself. It hits me like a blow to the chest, winding me, forcing me to gasp for air. I'm in love with Jason. Crazy, desperate, all-consuming, wonderful, wonderful love.

And it's freaking tearing me up inside.

I should be swinging from the trees, bursting with euphoria, lighting up the sky with my bliss. Instead, I fight the tears threatening to spill over, threatening to make me look even more ridiculous in front of this guy.

"I'm-I'm sorry." I try to smile but I must look like I've swallowed a glass of lime juice.

"Is it your ex? Are you still in love with him?"

. I clamp my teeth and shake my head. "It's someone else. Someone who doesn't know I'm in love with him." My lips begin to tremble, and I scrunch my eyes shut.

"Look. I know I'm just some guy who you've decided not to date—"

I snap my head up to look at him. "Oh, no. Cameron, it's not like that." Even though it so totally is. There's no point making this any worse than it already is for the poor guy.

"Let me finish?"

I give a short, sharp nod. Allowing him to say what he wants to say is the least I can do after what I've put him through tonight. All for nothing.

"If you love this guy, really love him, tell him. Love doesn't come around a whole lot. If you find it, you've got to grab it while you can."

I search his eyes and detect a deep sadness. It's clear he's lost someone he loved. I swallow down my own pain and try out a watery smile. "You're a really great guy, Cameron. Do you know that?"

He lifts his shoulders in a modest shrug. "I do my best."

"I'm sorry I'm not the girl for you."

"Yeah. Me too."

As I take the slow trek back to my apartment, my heart sits heavy. How can I tell Jason how I feel about him when I know he doesn't feel the same way? Sure, he's told me he has faith in me, and it's obvious he cares. But love?

Love is a whole other planet.

And right now, that planet is populated by one very sad, very dateless girl.

Chapter 23

I stumble through the following day at High Tea, dragging my heart with a big, fake smile painted on my face. Thank God it's Sunday, our busiest day, so I don't get too much spare time to wallow in my abject misery.

I heard Jason come home late last night as I lay in my bed, my brain whirring. I tried to sleep. I think I managed about an hour or two sometime around three. Today, I'm really a zombie masquerading as a girl, with bags under my eyes I could use to go away to college.

Although Cameron told me last night not to let love slip through my fingers, I know I lack the courage to tell Jason how I feel.

I mean, how can I ever tell him? My friend, my roommate. The guy who's never lost for a date on a Saturday night. Or any night of the week, when I think about it.

It'll mean the end of our friendship, the end of us sharing an apartment. And I'm doing my very best to hold onto it all right now.

I lock the door once the last customers of the day have left and trudge slowly to the kitchen. I'm surprised to find both Bailey and Paige, talking in quiet tones by the walk-in pantry.

"Hi," I say as I walk over to them. "When did you two get here? I didn't expect either of you today."

"Sophie! It's great to see you," Paige says. "We snuck in a few minutes ago."

I stand back and take in her girth. By the looks of her, I can't imagine Paige being able to "snuck" anywhere. "Large" doesn't begin to describe her belly, but then she is carrying a set of twins in there, which is something so incredible and beautiful, I find my eyes welling with tears.

There's an outside chance I'm a touch overly emotional today.

"It's great to see you, too," I manage once I've collected myself enough to speak. "How are the babies cooking in there?"

"They seem to have settled down into more of a groove, now, but oh, my back kills me by the end of the day. And look at my feet!"

I notice her feet are swollen up like a couple of pink grapefruits.

She places her hand on her belly. "They tell me it's perfectly normal when you're in your final trimester."

Bailey smiles at her friend and business partner. "You're a total trooper, Paige. How's today gone?" she asks me.

I want to tell her it's been like wading through a quagmire of thick, unrelenting heartache with every step I take, and that I've had to fight not to tear up whenever anyone says a kind word to me. I don't. Mainly because that would be melodramatic and totally inappropriate in the workplace, but also because the last thing I want to do is go into the whole Jason saga with my bosses.

Or anyone, really.

"It's been a good day. Busy, but not full. You know, the usual Sunday," I reply.

Bailey and Paige share a look before Bailey says, "Shall we take a seat? We've got to discuss some things."

A few moments later, the three of us sit around one of the tables.

Bailey lets out a puff of air. "Look, Sophie. There's no easy way to say this, so I'm just going to come out with it."

A sense of impending doom seeps up my legs as I look from Bailey to Paige and back again. "Okay."

She clears her throat and continues. "We all know High Tea hasn't been doing well. The thing is, Paige and I met with our accountant last week." She looks at Paige, her face creased with emotion. "We're . . . We've got to . . ." She breaks off.

"What Bailey's trying to say is that our accountant is concerned that things haven't improved at High Tea. She suggested we cut our losses and close it down."

My eyes grow wide and my voice is breathless as I repeat, "Close High Tea down? Y-you want to close High Tea down?"

"You're doing a fantastic job, honey, so please know this is nothing to do with you," Bailey says. "But with the way this place is sucking money from the café, we decided we need to listen to her advice."

My pulse is about to get a speeding ticket it's racing so darn fast. "But-but I came up with a proposal. I have a plan to save High Tea."

"We know you do, and it's such a great idea." As she looks at me, Bailey's expression is one of sadness and regret. "We're so sorry, Sophie. We know how much this job means to you."

My job. I'm losing my job. For some inexplicable reason, that fact had evaded me until this moment.

"We've got bookings for the next week which we will honor, but we plan on the fourteenth being High Tea's last day."

"The fourteenth," I echo. "Last day."

"We want you to know you've done a fantastic job, Sophie. Of course your barista job at the café is totally safe," Bailey says. "We'll write you an awesome reference if you decide to look for another manager's position elsewhere, and we'll pay you out to the end of the month. It's the least we can do."

The least you can do is keep High Tea open so my entire life doesn't completely implode.

I don't say it. I'm too numb.

LATER, I sit in my car, staring at the blank wall of the parking building in front of me.

High Tea is closing down.

No more Weekend Manager's job.

Just as it always is when anything happens in my life, big or small, my first thought is to share this devastating news with Jason. A lump forms in my throat as I realize I can't share this with him. I don't trust myself to be around him, let alone sob on his broad shoulders. I would end up blurting out my feelings, make a total fool of myself, and then life as I know it would be gone.

And it's already halfway gone as it is.

So, thirty minutes later, I find myself pulling up outside Darcy and Erin's apartment. It's five o'clock on a damp and miserable rainy Sunday, so the chances both Darcy and Erin are home, curled up in front of Netflix, is pretty high.

I compose myself as best I can before I press the buzzer, and wait until I hear a familiar voice say, "Darcy and Erin's Morgue. You stab 'em, we slab 'em."

I go to laugh at my friend's overdone joke, but it comes out more as a half-choked sob than anything resembling real laughter. "Hi, it's me," I say, but it sounds weird, strangled, like I've been possessed by the spirit of Fozzy Bear with a cold.

"Look, if you're that weirdo from yesterday, wanting to inspect our refrigerator to make sure it's cold enough, you can take a leap off a cliff. A very high one." The static disappears, and I know Darcy's hung up.

I press the button again. This time when she answers, I'm better prepared. "Darce, it's me, Sophie."

"Oh, thank God! I thought it was someone else. I'll buzz you in."

The door pops open and I push through it. I climb the two flights to their apartment, and by the time Darcy swings her door open, my resolve to stay strong has well and truly left the building. I crumple into a flood of tears.

"Soph, babe. What's going on?"

"I've-I've lost my job," I splutter.

"Oh, Sophie. That's terrible." She wraps her arm around me and leads me into the living room where Erin is looking at me, concern written across her face.

"What's happened?" she asks in alarm.

I plunk myself down heavily on the sofa, still warm from where the girls had been sitting only moments before. I look up at the TV and see a paused episode of *Gilmore Girls*, the actresses' familiar faces beaming out at me.

Darcy sits on one side of me as Erin perches on the other.

"Tell us what happened," Darcy says.

So, I tell them about the impending demise of High Tea. Well, in between sobs, that is.

"Oh, honey, that's terrible," Erin says.

Darcy shakes her head. "And you'd done all that research and put that awesome proposal together, too."

"They were really nice about it, and they said they'll pay me out to the end of the month. They said I can stay on as a barista at the café, but maybe I should find another job? Don't go back, and all that." I swallow as the reality of what losing High Tea really means hits me in the chest. "Oh, God. My siblings will force me into one of those internships. I'll have to move back home."

Darcy's hand flies to her mouth. "No!"

Erin shakes her head. "You don't have to do that. You're a fully grown woman. You can find another job, no problem. You're amazing. And if you move back home, you'll miss Jason too much."

Jason. I scrunch my eyes shut at the mention of his name, only for them to ping open a moment later when Darcy reaches across me to whack Erin on the arm. "Shut up, Erin!"

Erin's eyes bulge. "What? What did I say? She will miss Jas. They've been roomies for*ever*. They're as thick as thieves, as Mom says. Whatever 'thick' means. You know, I've never really understood that expression? What does a 'thick thief' look like, anyway?"

Darcy glares at her. "Not helping right now, Erin." She rubs my back as I keep my eyes lowered.

"What? Why?" Erin's tone turns to exasperation when she says, "Will someone *please* tell me what's going on here?"

I lift my eyes to hers and let out a puff of air. It's time to come clean. "I've got a bit of a crush on Jason." I bite my lip as I wait for her response.

She surprises me. "A crush? Is that what you kids are calling it these days?"

"Erin, you're only six and a half months older than Sophie," Darcy protests.

Erin ignores her. Her voice is soft when she says, "It's love, isn't it, Soph? You love Jason."

A deep and true warmth spreads through my chest, and I nod as I try in vain to swallow that darn persistent lump in my throat. "How-how did you know?"

She lifts a shoulder. "I've known for ages."

It's my eyes' turn to bulge. "You have?"

She nods. "Oh, yeah. It's as obvious to me as balls on a pig."

Darcy pulls a face. "Erin, that's gross."

"What? I work for a sports team. Jocks, every last one of them. You think some of that doesn't rub off onto me? You knew, too, right, Darce?"

"Only because Sophie told me."

"And you didn't think to share that with your bestie-slash-roommate?"

"I couldn't. I promised not to. And anyway, shouldn't we be focusing on Sophie here?"

I give them both a watery smile. "It's okay, girls. I'm probably more comfortable talking about pigs' balls, anyway." My attempt at humor has my friends smiling. But it becomes clear they're not done with me yet.

"How long have you known you're in love with him?" Erin asks.

My chest aches as I think of Jason. "It's been creeping up on me for so long, it's hard to say."

"But you feel best when you're with him, when it's just the two of you together, hanging out or having fun. Right?" Erin asks.

I nod. My mind flashes to all the time we spend together: playing video games, chatting over drinks, even watching rugby together. I feel like myself around him in a way I've never felt around another guy before. I can be me. And it feels so right.

Erin places her hand on my arm. "Honey? Have you talked to Jason about how you feel?"

"Talk to him? Are you *insane*?" I snap. "Sorry, sorry. I know he doesn't feel the same way."

Erin's eyebrows ping up. "Do you actually know that?"

I nod grimly. "I do. He's dating Megan, anyway. They went to Chez Pierre."

"Chez Pierre? Ouch," Darcy says.

I slump my shoulders. "See? It's a hopeless situation."

Erin shifts her position on the sofa arm. "If you're not going to talk to Jason about it, what are you planning to do?"

"Sit it out and hope it passes quickly."

"Treat him like he's the flu," Darcy says.

"Like the flu," I echo. "Oh, and definitely avoid him, particularly when he's in nothing but a towel."

"Oh, I knew that would happen one day. Didn't I always say that? Inevitable," Darcy says.

"What did you do about Cameron?" Erin asks.

"I put him out of his misery last night. I had to. How could I date him knowing I was in love with someone else? It wouldn't be right."

"You made the right call," Erin says softly. She springs up. "I'm getting you a drink. Chardonnay, I assume?"

I nod. "A super large one, please."

A glass or three later (not that I'm telling), conversation eventually turns from Jason back to the fate of my job at High Tea.

"Why don't you go out with a bang? Give it all you've got?" Darcy suggests.

"Yes! That would be amazing," Erin confirms.

"Go out with a bang? You mean go postal and blow High Tea up?" I reply with a sardonic smile.

"Well, there's always that as a last resort," Erin jokes. At least, I think it's a joke. Right now, my judgment is seriously impaired by the amount of emotional upheaval I'm going through. And the Chardonnay. Definitely the Chardonnay.

"It means do what you suggested in your proposal. Get some music in there, lighten the mood, bring the Cozy Cottage feel to the place," Darcy says. "Isn't that what you told them was missing?"

"I'd have to hire musicians and do a bunch of stuff. They'll never go for it." I shake my head, feeling thoroughly depleted.

"They will if it costs them nothing," Darcy says, her eyes bright. "I've got an idea."

Chapter 24

Five days is not a whole lot of time. This is something I've learned all too well now.

I've taken Darcy's idea to "go out with a bang" and run with it at full tilt. If High Tea is going to meet its demise, it's going to do it in style.

I got Paige and Bailey on board easily when I explained how little it would cost to deliver my vision. I suspect a healthy dollop of guilt on their part that I had the Weekend Manager job for such short a time helped push them over the decision-making edge, too.

But hey, whatever works, right?

Although Mondays and Tuesdays are my days off, this week I spent them working in High Tea, and I threw my everything into it . . . with a little help from my fabulous friends. Naturally.

Darcy is getting a bunch of ornate, gilded mirrors from her mom's interior décor store, which we plan on hanging on the walls to make High Tea feel more spacious and luxurious.

Erin went to work on Monday morning and sent an email out to all the team's players, strongly suggesting they treat their W.A.G.s— wives and girlfriends, although hopefully the players have either a wife *or* a girlfriend because that's a minefield we don't want to get stuck in—to High Tea. She worked out that Sunday is exactly six months since Valentine's Day, so she called it the "Be My Demi-Valentine High Tea Celebration." Genius. So far, we've had bookings for seven W.A.G.s and counting.

Did I mention how much I love my friends?

As well as increasing the warmth of the Cozy Cottage Café while making it feel classier, the other part of my master plan is to have live music to make the High Tea experience fun as well as fancy and delicious.

Operation: Fun and Fancy is underway! (And yes, I did just go there.)

So, after having successfully avoided Jason but for a (thankfully fully clothed) "ships in the night" hallway incident early yesterday morning, I feel like I've got a bunch of over-exuberant bell ringers clanging around inside my chest when I stroll into the kitchen, feigning breeziness.

"Hey, Jas." I keep my voice as bright and breezy as I can manage, as though seeing him doesn't make my heart beat right out of my chest and the butterflies in my belly morph into fully grown eagles.

He's got his back to me, leaning over his breakfast cereal as he reads his phone. He turns to look at me over his shoulder in that sexy, smoldering Keanu Reeves in *Point Break* way he does so very well. I'm forced to clench my hands at my sides to stop from hurtling myself at him in a rush of lust and love, a thoroughly potent concoction by anyone's standards.

Keep your nerve, Sophie, keep your nerve…

He runs his fingers through his thick dark hair and flashes me one of his toe-curling smiles. "Good morning, McCarthy." He runs his eyes over me. "I see you're pulling off the girl next door look perfectly today. Very sexy."

Seriously, no woman should have to deal with this level of temptation over the breakfast table.

I pull nervously at my T-shirt. "Err, thanks."

"I've barely seen you this week. What's been happening?"

I walk around to the other side of the breakfast bar. Strategically placed furniture is my friend right now, and I need all the support I can get to keep me from blurting out my feelings. "Oh, you know, this and that. I've been super busy."

"Want some coffee to go with your 'this and that?' There's some fresh in the pot."

"Thanks." On shaking legs, I turn and fix myself a coffee, then take it back to the breakfast bar.

"Why are you up so early on your day off?" he asks.

"I'm working on a project."

"Ah, your 'make High Tea more profitable' project. Nice. How's that going, anyway?"

"I guess you could say I've got one final shot at that this week."

"Oh?"

I tell him about how Bailey and Paige are closing High Tea down, how they've agreed to let me deliver my vision for its final two days this weekend, and how Darcy and Erin have been helping me out with their contacts and ideas.

Once I've finished, he looks at me for a while before he says, "You're the bravest person I know, McCarthy. Do you know that?"

Embarrassed, I shake my head. "I'm just a girl about to lose a job she loves and trying to feel better about it. I'm not especially brave."

"Ah, yeah, you are. Let's look at the facts." He begins to count points off on his fingers. "You told your meddling siblings to go stick it when they were putting all this pressure on you to fall into line. I know Sean and your sisters, so I know how brave that is. Number two, you're going on all these dates to find a good guy, which is harder than you thought, right?"

"Much harder."

"But still you put yourself out there, and now you've found one."

I snap my eyes to his as my heart hammers in my chest. Does he know how I feel about him? Is this the big reveal where we tell each other we love one another and then fall into one another's arms?

Or am I just deluding myself? Yup, probably.

"I, ah—" I mutter and then clear my throat as my cheeks flame red hot. "What do you mean?"

Jason narrows his eyes at me. "Cameron Lewis."

Cameron. Of course. As my heart sinks, I paste on a smile. "No one. No one at all."

"There's no way a guy like Cameron Lewis would fail the Pact Vetting Phase."

"No, no, you're right. He totally passed. The girls loved him. The thing is, I—"

He puts his hand in the air in the "stop" sign. "No details required." He folds one of his fingers and his thumb down so he has three fingers left in the air. "Three, you chased your dream of running High Tea when Sean and your sisters told you it wasn't the right move. Sure, it doesn't look like it's going to work out, but that doesn't even matter."

The sudden change in subject back to my alleged bravery almost gives me whiplash.

"Actually, it kinda does matter."

He shakes his head. "No, it doesn't. What matters is you wanted it and you went after it. If that's not brave, McCarthy, I don't know what is." He leans back in his seat as he studies my face and says, "Accept it: you're brave. And I think you're amazing."

Seriously? Why does he have to go saying things like that? Doesn't he know it makes me love him even more?

My heart is pounding like a drum in my throat. If only he knew the truth. When it comes to Jason Christie, I'm not in the least bit brave. In fact, I'm a complete and utter coward.

Instead, I simply smile at him then lower my eyes and take a sip of my coffee. "Um, thanks." I take a breath and then look back up at him. For a moment, as I look into his beautiful brown eyes, I feel as though I can tell him. I can tell him how much he means to me, how much I want to be with him, how much I love him.

How much I want him to love me, too.

But this is Jason. He's my roommate, he's one of my besties. He's never been serious about a girl in his life. What would make *me* any different?

He narrows his eyes. "What's going on with you? You seem all pensive or something. Is everything okay?"

I've got to keep these feelings inside. I'd rather have him in my life as a friend, than not at all.

"I'm fine, but I do have a weird favor to ask," I say.

He shoots me his cheekiest grin, and my heart expands. "Weird favors are the best kind. What is it?"

I clear my throat. "I need some musicians to play at High Tea over the weekend, and I remember at karaoke Megan mentioned she and her brothers were in a seventies cover band."

"The Mersons. They're like the von Trapps, *without* the Nazis." His eyes are bright.

"That's right."

"You want me to ask her if she could perform?"

"Would that be okay? She's such an amazing singer, and I really think her band's style of music would totally work there. They could perform acoustically so people could still talk without having to shout."

He shrugs. "No problem. Leave it with me."

I release a rush of air. "Really? Thank you so much, Jas. You don't know how much this means to me."

He smiles and holds my gaze for a fraction too long for comfort. My comfort. "I think I do."

I avert my eyes. "Great. Well, I've got to go," I reply briskly. "Darcy's turning up with a bunch of mirrors this morning, and I've got so many things to get done."

As I collect my things and leave our apartment, I allow myself one final glance in Jason's direction. He's in the same spot at the kitchen counter, reading something on his phone. As I'm about to tear my eyes away, he looks up at me, and my heart skips a beat.

I want to say it. Oh, so much.

Instead, I smile and say, "Thanks again," and close the front door behind me.

⸺

FINALLY, after working harder all week than I've ever worked in my entire life, the second to last day of High Tea's life arrives. I look around the room at what we've achieved in such a short amount of time. The mirrors—which took me, Darcy, Bailey, and Alex a major effort and quite a few colorful words to hang—lend an air of luxury and sophistication to the space that was missing before. With her designer's eye, Darcy's mom helped us work out where to put them, and she even lent us some music-themed scatter cushions, covered with treble clefs and quavers and illustrations of musicians.

While we were working, Bailey remembered she had a couple of boxes of fairy lights from when Cassie and Will got married at High Tea, before this building was even called High Tea. They are now adorning the walls and hanging from the ceiling, making the place positively glow and sparkle. Quite literally.

Looking around me, I feel both a strong sense of achievement and one of impending loss. These two days are the last for Cozy Cottage High Tea. Even though the place looks better than it ever has before, I know the dream will be over soon, and I'll have to face my new reality.

"You've done such an amazing job, Sophie."

I turn to see Bailey, her eyes soft, her smile warm. "We all did."

"It was you. This is your vision. The mirrors remind me of a gorgeous bistro in Paris I went to years ago with my fiancé."

Thor in Paris, huh? Talk about heightening the romance quota of the world's most romantic city. "I didn't know you and Ryan had gone to France together."

She presses her lips together as she shakes her head. "This was before Ryan, when I was engaged to Josh's brother, Dan. He died before we got married."

"Oh, Bailey. I had no idea. I'm so sorry."

"Thank you. You know, when I first met Jason, he reminded me of Dan. I admit, it kind of freaked me out."

Realization dawns on me. "He mentioned you acted weird around him. I told him it was all in his head. He's used to women fawning over him, you see, not running the other direction."

She lets out a soft laugh. "I think a girl could do a lot worse than him."

I flash my eyes to hers. "I guess, although he's too much of a player for any sane woman to get serious about."

She shrugs. "Maybe."

Maybe? What does that mean? Of course he's too much of a player. Everyone knows that.

I open my mouth to question her, but Bailey's attention has been diverted to the door. "Look, the band's arrived. They sounded so good at the Friday Night Jam. The audience loved them."

As part of the deal to lure Megan and her band to play at High Tea, we gave them the chance to play to a packed audience at the Cozy Cottage last night. They brought the house down with their covers of Blondie, Elton John, and ABBA, although Darcy and Erin were not so secretly annoyed they did such an amazing job of their favorite 'The Winner Takes It All.'

I pull the double doors open wide and greet Megan and her really rather good-looking brothers. The Mersons were blessed with a good gene pool, that's for sure. If I wasn't so hung up on Jason . . . I let out a heavy sigh. What's the point? There's no use even looking at another guy until I've managed to extricate Jason from my heart.

And doing just that is the reason why I've decided I need to move out of my apartment. Seeing Jason every day, knowing he will never be mine, no matter how great a friend he is, seeing him bring Megan or the next girl home? I know it'll tear my heart in two.

I'm no masochist. I can't be around that.

What I need is a fresh slate, a new beginning, to turn over a new leaf. Yup, I need every cliché in the book, and I need them to happen now. Then I can press on with the utterly gut-wrenching business of getting over him.

Because I know getting over Jason Christie will be the hardest thing I'll ever have to do.

"Oh, Sophie," Megan says as she gives me a quick hug. "Thank you so much for this, and for last night. We had so much fun."

"Thank *you* for playing for us on such short notice. You guys are awesome."

She gives a flick of her wrist. "I just had to juggle some shifts at the hospital. No big deal. Now, we're going fully acoustic except for the microphone, right?"

"Right. Fun and lively, but we still want people to be able to talk."

The band sets about getting themselves organized, and I spend the next hour before we open to customers giving instructions to staff and making sure every last detail is in place. Alex is here to serve, his cheeky grin firmly in place, ready to charm the customers.

When Erin and Darcy arrive, a large bunch of gorgeous flowers for me in hand, I know it's only a few minutes to opening.

I stand at the podium, ready to welcome our first group of customers as the band begins to play. The music is perfect, their acoustic rendition of David Bowie's "Changes" hitting absolutely the right note. Pun intended.

The place hums with customers, and before long it's halfway through High Tea's penultimate day. I've just finished seating a group of Erin's W.A.G.s, with their perfect grooming, cow-length eyelashes, and suspiciously full and pouty lips, when I spot Jason at the podium. My heart almost leaps out of my chest at the unexpected sight of him in his black V-neck T-shirt and perfectly fitted jeans. His dark stubble-lined face lights up when his eyes land on me, and I do my best not to read anything into it.

"You've outdone yourself, McCarthy. This place is outstanding." He leans in and brushes his lips against my cheek.

My skin tingles where he touched me. "I had help," I protest, but inside, I'm beaming. "Megan's band is great. Thank you so much for setting it up for me."

He glances over in her direction and gives her a little wave. "No problem. Now, I brought some people."

I look at the group waiting behind him, chatting to one another, and I twist my mouth. "I'm so sorry, Jas, but we're actually fully booked all day. First time since I started in here, actually." I allow myself a small but triumphant smile.

"In that case, you'll be happy to know I've got a booking. Actually, I've got two."

My eyebrows ping up. "Two?"

He lifts his shoulders as his face quirks into a fresh smile. "What can I say? I'm a high tea junkie."

I scrunch up my nose. "I don't think that's a thing."

"Oh, it's a thing." His lips twitch. "I've got a booking today, and one for tomorrow. Two sets of people, two high teas. Today's booking is under the name 'Doug Ross.'"

I shake my head. "Why Doug Ross? Do you have a secret identity I don't know about?"

"Sophie McCarthy, I refuse to believe you don't know who Doug Ross is."

I shrug. "I don't, but I have the feeling I'm about to be enlightened."

"George Clooney played Doug Ross in *E.R.* I credit my career choice to him, actually."

"And you fancy yourself as George Clooney, too, right?"

He waggles his eyebrows at me. "I guess you'll have to ask the ladies about that. Now, some of us have just come off a long shift saving lives and we're all super hungry, so could you please find our booking so we can get on with eating ridiculously small but delicious things?"

A bubble of laughter builds up inside me. "You do realize there is a lot of food in these high teas, right? Coming today and tomorrow you're not going to go hungry, that's for sure."

He taps his taut belly. "I need some fattening up."

Yeah, because *no one* wants to see a hot guy's perfect six-pack.

I will myself not to think of him in just his towel and instead concentrate as I run my finger over the list until I spot Jason's— Doug Ross's—booking.

"You've got a booking for ten people, Mr. Ross." I collect the menus and lead Jason and his friends to one of the tables. As I hand Jason his menu, I quietly say, "Thanks for this."

Our gazes lock, his eyes intense. "Anything for you, McCarthy."

I swallow. Anything?

Someone at the table says something to him and he tears his attention away. Me? I'm torn between feeling so light and happy I could float on air and wanting to curl up in a ball and eat chocolate and chips for the rest of my life. "Conflicted" doesn't even begin to describe the churn of emotions running through me right now.

I spend the next hour working my butt off, trying to make the day extra special for every person who walks through the door. No matter how hard I work, I still manage occasional furtive glances at Jason. Sometimes he's talking, sometimes he's laughing, sometimes he looks over at me and smiles. And even though I try with all my might, I can't stop my heart from swelling each and every time.

Chapter 25

I was too exhausted to even contemplate going to karaoke with the girls last night. Instead, I finished up late at High Tea, went straight home, and flopped into bed.

And now, after a long but erratic sleep, my head filled to the brim with a cacophony of thoughts, I find myself back here on High Tea's final day.

Just as I did yesterday, I stand in the center of the room and take a long look around me. This is it, the final day, the end of High Tea —and the end of my Cozy Cottage journey.

It's certainly been a week of big decisions.

"I really wish you weren't leaving us, Sophie," Bailey says as she and Paige weave through the tables toward me. "We are so sad to lose you."

Paige shakes her head, her face drawn. "We'll never be able to replace you. You've been a part of the Cozy Cottage from the beginning, before even me."

My chest tightens. It's true, I have been here from the beginning. As a new graduate, I walked into the café and fell in love with the place. I met the happy, smiling Bailey, and she told me she was looking for a barista as she handed me my very first slice of Cozy

Cottage cake. It sure wasn't my last, and the rest is history, a history I'm glad I was a part of.

A history that now can be only that.

"I guess with High Tea closing, it seems like the right time to go," I say. "You know what? Managing High Tea every weekend has been my dream. I know things haven't worked out the way we wanted them to, but I've loved every minute."

"Oh, stop it." Paige fans her face as tears spill down her cheeks.

"I also want to thank you both for giving me the chance to show you my High Tea vision this weekend. It, well, it meant a lot to me." My voice has begun to quaver, my throat hot and tight.

"It's beautiful, Sophie, and being fully booked has been amazing, too," Bailey says, her own eyes brimming with tears.

Paige wipes her tears away. "You mean *over*booked. You had to bring some of the tables in from the café yesterday."

"I had people standing to drink their coffee in the café," Bailey adds. "It was a good problem to have."

"There you all are," a deep voice says behind us.

We turn to see Alex standing in the entrance to the kitchen, his hair tied back, his handsome face beaming in a broad smile. "You all ready for the grand finale?"

I turn back and look from Paige to Bailey, and I can see in their eyes that today is tough on them, too. "I guess we are?"

Bailey presses her lips together and nods. "Let's give this place the sendoff it deserves."

And what a sendoff. Megan and the band play throughout the day, we have a seemingly endless stream of customers, and we're so busy I've barely got the chance to think about anything else.

Well, almost.

Erin and Darcy arrive for their final Cozy Cottage High Tea indulgence in the middle of the day, and I take them to my favorite table for two in the room, right by the window.

"How are you holding up?" Erin asks as she takes her seat.

"I'm trying not to think about it. *Any* of it," I reply stiffly. "Okay. Here are your menus. The handsome Alex will be your server today, and he'll be over to take your order shortly."

"Alex is fun, and super cute," Erin says with a grin. "Don't you think, Darce?"

Darcy gives a shrug. "Sure, he might be pretty to look at, but I knew him in high school, remember? I don't exactly feel all warm and fuzzy about that guy."

"What did he do to you? You've never told us," Erin says.

"Let's just say I wish we'd formed the No More Bad Dates Pact a long, long time ago," she replies elusively.

"So, will you be asking us to vet him sometime soon?" I tease.

Darcy fixes me with her stare. "That'd be a hard no."

"What's a hard no?" Alex asks as he materializes at my side. "Hello, ladies. You're looking particularly stunning today."

As Erin beams at him and Darcy harrumphs and crosses her arms, I respond to a customer waving at me from another table before I make my way back to the podium to greet our next group of customers.

"We really must stop meeting for high tea like this, McCarthy," a voice I know so well says.

I steel myself for a major heart contraction before I look up from my list of bookings into Jason's eyes. Just as he was yesterday, he looks impossibly Keanu Reeves handsome, only this time he's in a crisp white button up shirt, showing off his tan skin and dark hair.

"After today, that won't be a problem." I try out a smile. Judging by the way Jason's own cheeky version drops, my bet is it comes out more as a grimace.

"You doing okay there, champ?"

I lift my shoulders. "It's a tough day."

"Let me make it all up to you when you're home tonight."

My voice is a touch breathless when I reply, "Sure." My mind goes to a place Jason didn't intend. And I'm not going to tell exactly where it goes, but let's just say it's not the sort of thing you'd tell your mom about—and leave it at that.

"Now. Focus, McCarthy. Today's booking is under 'O'Leary' for three o'clock. We should be the final booking of the day."

As I scan the sheet for the name with my finger, I ask, "Why 'O'Leary,' exactly, Jas? Let me guess. Another famous TV doctor?"

"Oh, it's his idea of a joke."

I snap my head up at the familiar voice to see Mom waiting at Jason's side, her eyes bright, her face glowing.

"James 'Big Jim' O'Leary was an Irish mob boss in Chicago back in the 1800s," she continues as though she's swallowed a history book. "We're the 'O'Learys' today. Your Jason here fancies himself as a bit of a jokester, *dote*."

My Jason? My cheeks heat right up. I walk around the podium to give Mom a hug. "Hey, Mom. I didn't know you were coming today."

It was too hard for me to admit defeat to my family, especially after making my big announcement about my new career direction when I first got the High Tea job. Although I hadn't stuck around at the Mandatory McCarthy Meal on Thursday night to listen to the "I told you so's" from Sean, Caitlin, Fiona, and Abigail, I had told them of High Tea's unfortunate demise. Until I looked at my mom's beaming face in this very moment, I didn't think I wanted any of them here today.

Mom takes my hands in hers, and that emotional lump that keeps pestering my throat turns up, making my eyes hot and gummy. "We're proud of you, love. All of us, even your brother and sisters, who I know can be right bossy when they get stuck on something."

I press my lips together and give a small nod. "Right bossy" is exactly what they can be.

"We wouldn't have known you were doing all this if it wasn't for your Jason here."

There it is again: *my Jason*. Despite every reason not to, I lift my eyes to his, and my heart skips a beat. His eyes are full of kindness as he looks back at me.

"This place looks just wonderful, *mo stoirín*. And the music! Who would have thought to have lively music playing at high tea?"

I try to blink away the tears that have welled in my eyes, but one of them evades capture and slides down my cheek. "Thanks, Mom."

She rubs my arm. "Now, now. Don't go getting all sad about it. You've got an important job to do today."

"I know."

"Now, where are you sitting us? We'll need a good-sized table."

"You will?" I ask as the door swings open. I look over and blink at the gaggle of people. *My* people. My family, every last one of them.

"Hey, sis," Abigail says as Sean nods at me and Fiona and Caitlin plant kisses on my cheeks.

"Hello, love," Dad says, bringing up the rear. He whistles as he looks around. "This place looks incredible. You've zhuzhed it up a bit, haven't you?"

A giggle of surprised happiness and nervousness bubbles up inside me—happiness because I love my family and Jason brought them to be here today, and nervousness because, well, they're my family and having them here showcases my failure to 'do something important' with my life.

"We have zhuzhed it up, Dad. You're right." I echo the expression he's used since we were kids.

I look around at my family's faces, and at Jason, who has slunk to the back of the "O'Leary" mafia pack. Choking with emotion once more, I barely manage to say, "Thanks for coming, guys. It-it means a lot to me."

Mom waves my comment away. "We've all come with a fierce appetite today."

"She told us all to skip lunch," Sean complains.

"We're starving!" Abigail adds.

I lead them to our largest table by the whitewashed brick fireplace at the back of the room then pass out their menus. Alex comes to greet them, and Mom goes supersonic Irish on us all in her excitement. "Oh, *dote*. It's grand to see you. Grand!"

"What are you doing here, Alex?" Caitlin asks. "The last Auntie Margie told us, you were in India doing amazing things."

Alex's smile is smooth when he replies, "Now I'm here doing amazing things with Sophie at Cozy Cottage High Tea. Hasn't she done an incredible job with this place?"

Nice change of topic there, Alex.

My family murmurs their consensus.

"What's good here?" Sean asks as he peruses his menu.

"All of it." Jason's voice is firm as he takes his seat next to Mom. "Go for the most expensive option, Sean, and order one for everyone. Your treat, right?"

As Sean begrudgingly confirms it is indeed his treat, I beam at Jason.

Seriously. Could he get any more freaking perfect?

At closing time, the only customers left in the room are Erin, Darcy, Jason, and my family, all of whom look thoroughly well-fed and satisfied. Megan and her brothers are packing up their instruments and Bailey and Paige's husbands, Ryan and Josh, have arrived along with Cassie and husband, Will, and Marissa and boyfriend, Nash—the initial four members of the One Last First Date Pact, the inspiration for our own dating pact.

The front door is locked, and it's party time. Cozy Cottage High Tea is now officially no more, and it's not an exaggeration for me to say I feel like a small part of me has gone with it (okay, maybe it is a little over the top, but this feeling really sucks).

I lean up against the wall between the large mirrors we hung only days before. I have a sunken feeling as I look around the familiar faces, the faces I won't see as often anymore. The faces that have made my Cozy Cottage world what it's been.

I feel Jason's presence beside me before I hear him say, "A penny for them?"

"Oh, I'm feeling a little sad, that's all."

"Saying goodbye is hard."

I lift my eyes to his before I look quickly away. I've not had the courage to tell Jason I plan on moving out yet. I'm not sure how he's going to take it.

There's a clinking sound of spoon against glass. Bailey has ensured we all have a glass of champagne in our hands, and once she has everyone's attention, she begins to speak. "High Tea was Paige's and my baby, and more recently, it had become Sophie's baby, too. Together, I think we created something special here."

There's a murmur of agreement. "It was just a shame not more Aucklanders thought that, too," she adds and a ripple of laughter rolls through the room. "Sophie, thank you for everything you've done. The Cozy Cottage will miss you, but we wish you all the best in your new, exciting career at your sister's company."

I can feel Jason's questioning gaze boring into me, but I don't turn to look.

"So, I ask that you all raise your glasses and give a final toast to Cozy Cottage High Tea. We're going to miss it here."

"To Cozy Cottage High Tea," people repeat.

I feel Jason's hand on my arm, and I scrunch my eyes shut, knowing what's to come. "You're taking the internship at Babyness?"

I bite my lip and turn to face him. "It's better than working for boring lawyers, don't you think?" My attempt to make light of it falls on deaf ears.

He knits his brows together. "Why?"

"Because I realized Sean and my sisters are right. I need to do something with my life, Jas. Managing High Tea has shown me I'm capable of doing so much more. I've loved working here at the Cozy Cottage, but it feels right to move on. You're following your dream and becoming a doctor. I'm twenty-six next month, and I've done nothing with my life."

"That's crazy, Soph. You've done loads. And anyway, why are you listening to Sean? I'm sorry, I know he's your brother and all, but he's a total dick."

Despite it all, I bite back a smile. Jason never fails to have my back, and I love him for it.

And that's the biggest problem of them all.

"Sean might not be the easiest of brothers, it's true, but I know he's always trying to look out for me, to give me opportunities I wouldn't otherwise have. He may go about it in a domineering, OTT way—all my siblings do—but at his heart, he's a good guy and I know he loves me."

Jason shakes his head, his gaze not leaving my face. "Is it what you want, Soph?"

The tenderness in his voice has my heart contracting despite the heavy brick in the pit of my stomach. "What I want, I can't have, so I've got to go for the next best thing."

"And that's Baby-ness?"

I nod. "Caitlin's agreed to pay me a wage. It'll grow to a full-time salary once I'm up to speed with the business. She's going to mentor me. I'll learn a lot from her."

He studies my face for a beat, two. Eventually, he says, "Does this mean you're moving out of our apartment?"

I allow my shoulders to slump as I look down at my feet. "That's another thing I've got to do."

And then he does something I don't expect. Instead of telling me I'm crazy, he takes me by the hand and says, "Come with me."

"Where?" I ask, confused.

"Sophie McCarthy, for once in your life, can you do something I ask you to do without questioning it?"

His warm hand still holding mine, I scrunch up my nose and reply, "Okay. Just this once."

He leads the way out to the covered courtyard at the back of the room. It's empty but for some tables and chairs and fairy lights adorning the walls. Once in the middle of the space, he turns to face me and takes my other hand in his.

My heart is pounding like one of those huge drums at the back of an orchestra, and as I look up and see the intensity in his dark eyes, my breath hitches in my throat.

Doesn't he know what this is doing to me? To my heart?

"Erin told me you're not dating Cameron Lewis."

Confused by the unexpected change in topic, I say, "I . . . what?"

"Don't be annoyed with her. She slipped up and felt bad about it." He squeezes my hands. "Soph, did you ever wonder why I didn't come to his vetting that night?"

I shake my head. I had assumed he was on a date with Megan, but by the way he's looking at me right now, I'm not so sure.

"My fear was that I wouldn't find a reason for you *not* to date him. So, I stayed away."

I try to swallow, but my throat has dried up so much it's like a couple of pieces of parchment paper rubbing together. "Wh-why are you telling me this, Jas? I don't get what me not dating Cameron has to do with me working at Baby-ness and leaving the apartment."

His face lights up as he laughs. "I can't believe I'm going to say this, but you're leaving and to hell with our friendship."

I blink at him. "To hell with our friendship? Why? What are you talking about?"

"Soph, I know this is probably going to freak you out, and I get it. Really, I do. I've wrestled with this for so long now, and I've had enough of keeping this inside." He takes a deep breath, the emotion written across his face intensifying. "Sophie, I don't want to be friends with you anymore. I've-I've fallen in love with you." He holds his breath.

My jaw drops to the floor. "You're in love with me?" I feel like I'm in a dream, only the last thing I want to do is wake up from it.

He lets go of my hands and runs his fingers through his hair, clearly agitated. "I shouldn't have said anything. I'm so *stupid*." He rests his hands on the back of his neck and looks at me. "I've wrecked it, haven't I? I've totally wrecked the most important thing in my life. I can't believe I did this. What the hell was I thinking?"

"You're in love with me?" I repeat like I'm some sort of robot. "But . . . but Megan."

He shakes his head. "We broke up. She worked it out."

"Worked what out?" I breathe.

"That I was in love with someone else. They all work it out, eventually."

I blink at him, trying to process his words. The revolving door of girlfriends has all been because he's in love with *me*?

"Just forget it. Please." He bows his head and I reach out to touch his face. When he lifts his eyes to meet mine, I see the pain and anguish lurking beneath, and I know exactly what to do. It's what I've wanted to do—no, what I've *needed* to do—for so long.

I step closer to him and put my hand on his cheek. I push myself up onto the tips of my toes, and as I close my eyes, I brush my lips against his. He responds in an instant by wrapping his strong arms around me and pulling me close. And we kiss. And kiss. It's breathtakingly perfect, the kind of kiss you can easily live your whole life without experiencing. The kind of kiss you can only ever have with someone you love with all your heart and soul.

I pull back and look up into his eyes, my heart full. "Did you know that I am totally and completely in love with you, too, Jason Christie?"

The biggest grin I've ever seen busts out over his gorgeous face. "You have no idea how long I've wanted to hear you say that to me." He kisses me again, long and passionately, and if he wasn't holding me so tightly, I think I might have swooned right here in the courtyard.

"I love you, I love you, I love you, I love you," I say as I pepper his face with kisses. He laughs such a warm, deep laugh, it has electricity shooting through me.

He pulls back and looks deep into my eyes. "You know, a girl I know once told me she wants a guy to quote some lame Arianna Grande song to her and really, really mean it."

"That girl has got some good taste in music," I jest.

"That's debatable."

I punch him lightly on the arm.

"Sophie McCarthy? I am so in love with you, I can barely breathe."

I've never been this happy in my entire life. I bite my lip as tears prick my eyes. "Right back atcha, Christie."

Epilogue

"Where should we set up, Sophie?" a guy with curly brown hair and an open face asks me.

I point to the other side of the room. "Over there, please."

"You got it." He throws me a smile before he carries his large case to where I pointed.

I let out a contented sigh as I hold my warming Earl Grey tea in my hands. It's winter time, and I need what I can get to keep myself warm. I glance at the fireplace and write a mental note to get one of the guys to collect some more firewood. We need to keep everyone nice and toasty. This place is famous for its warm welcome, after all.

I feel a couple of hands snake around my middle and a head come to rest on my shoulder. "This place is better than ever."

His breath tickles my neck, and I spin around in his arms to face him. "Hello, there, Doctor Christie."

"Oh, say that again. I like the sound of that on your lips. And speaking of which…" he leans down and kisses me, right on my aforementioned lips.

"You know I'm holding hot tea here."

Jason beams back at me. "So, you're saying if I kiss you again, you'll be worried about spilling your tea?"

I laugh, and the happiness I have felt every day since Jason and I declared our mutual love bubbles to the surface. "Well, that and the fact we're at my workplace."

"All the more reason to kiss you, as far as I can tell."

"All right, you two. Break it up."

I drag my eyes from Jason and shoot Alex a contented smile. "Hey, Alex. You're back!"

Jason releases me from his grasp and we both greet him, me with a hug, and Jason with a handshake. I smile to myself as I think about how Jason had once been jealous of Alex, before he found out he was my sort-of cousin. If only I'd known how he felt about me then, I wouldn't have had to keep my love for him under wraps. My life would have been much more straightforward.

"How was your trip? You've got a great tan," I say.

"It was amazing," Alex replies. "I'll show you some photos tonight at the M.M.M."

"You've been roped into the Mandatory McCarthy Meal, have you?" I ask.

"Oh, yes," Alex replies. "Your mom made it pretty darn clear if I was in Auckland, I was coming to dinner."

"It'll be good to have you there, man," Jason says.

I hear the front door open and turn to see my two best friends stream in.

"OMG, Soph! I can't believe we're here." Erin collects me in a hug, and I breathe in her floral perfume.

"You belong here, girl," Darcy says. She greets Jason with a quick hug and then eyes Alex and says, "Alex."

"Darcy," he replies in an equally cold tone, although I think I detect a hint of humor in his voice.

Erin and I share a look. Really, whatever it was that happened between them, it was freaking years ago. #MoveOn

"Babe, we are so proud of you," Erin says.

"Full-time Manager of Cozy Cottage High Tea," Jason says. "Atta girl."

"Thanks." I glow at all my friends. Darcy, Erin, Alex, and of course, my love, Jason. They're all here for the grand re-opening, and I could not be more excited.

It's been almost five months since we closed, the day I thought my life would never be the same again. And it hasn't been, but in the very best way. Not only do I now have Jason, but thanks to an extremely well-timed and high-profile piece published in the city's largest paper the weekend High Tea closed, Bailey and Paige gave in to pressure to reopen. Apparently, High Tea's customers kicked up such a fuss, Bailey joked they needed to reopen just to shut them all up.

They invited yours truly to be at the helm, full time. No barista duties at the café next door. No working for nothing at Baby-ness, which is what I'd been doing for the last few months.

Sure, Caitlin had taught me a lot, and I actually ended up enjoying my time at Baby-ness, even growing to appreciate the importance of the breast pump market. But now, at High Tea, I get to live my dream. And I'm going to work my butt off to make this the best darn high tea experience in the city.

"There you are, *mo stoirín*," Mom says as she, Dad, and all my siblings and their families come streaming through the door.

"Hey, everyone," I say as I greet them all. "Thanks for coming."

"We've told everyone we know about the re-opening. I wouldn't be surprised if you'll be booked up to the end of time, *dote*," Mom says.

I laugh. "I hope you're right, Mom."

As my friends and family mingle, Sean puts his hand on my arm. "I'm really happy for you, Sophie."

My eyebrows ping up in surprise. Sean had been less than thrilled that I took the job at Caitlin's business. "Thank you, Sean. That means a lot."

"As the bard himself oft said, 'to thine own self be true,' and you are doing just that."

I grin at him. "Methink'st that bard of yours knows a thing or two."

He returns my smile. "That he does, Sophie. That he does."

With everyone happily mingling and the musicians setting themselves up, I walk out into the kitchen to do one final check before we open. Paige and her husband, Josh, are chatting with Bailey and Ryan, each of whom are holding a newborn baby in their arms.

"Oh, you two! They're beautiful." I peer at one baby's wrinkled little face and tickle her tummy. "Which one is this?"

"That's Tabitha, and Ryan's got Tilly," Paige says with a grin.

I smile at Ryan and stroke Tilly's head. "Well done, they're so gorgeous."

"Thanks," Josh replies with a beaming "new daddy" smile.

"Are you ready, Sophie?" Bailey asks.

I think of my friends and family, all here to support me. I think of Jason, whose faith in me has been unstinted, much like his love. "This is what I'm meant to do."

"I think you're right," Bailey replies.

"Before we open," I continue, "I want to say thank you so much for the opportunity. I cannot tell you how good it is to be back." I beam at Bailey and Paige, and they both smile back.

"That article caused such a furor! I can't tell you how many people complained that we'd closed," Paige says. "It turns out your ideas were just what the place needed. We're the ones who should be thanking you, Sophie."

"I told her that," Jason says, standing in the kitchen entranceway, and as our eyes meet, warmth spreads through me, filling my heart to the brim.

He walks over and puts his arm around my shoulder.

"Oh, you two look so good together," Paige says. "See? Another couple for whom a dating pact worked."

I shake my head. "Jason and I aren't a product of the No More Bad Dates Pact."

Paige shrugs. "Sure. But would you be together if you hadn't gone in on it?"

I look up at Jason and smile. In a weird kind of way, I guess the No More Bad Dates Pact worked out pretty darn well for me. Sure, no one ever officially vetted Jason, although Darcy certainly tried her best once we announced we were together. I told her it was a little too late for that, considering we'd fallen head over heels in love, and anyway, we all know Jason is one hundred percent my perfect match.

I'd wanted a Happy For Now, but I ended up finding my Happily Ever After.

THE END

Acknowledgments

It has been so much fun to revisit the girls of the Cozy Cottage Café and High Tea next door, and I'm so happy I got the chance to give Sophie her own book. When I wrote her in the final three books of the *Cozy Cottage Café* series, she screamed out at me to tell her story, so I'm thrilled to be able to give her the happily ever after she deserves.

As always, I've got a few people to thank (it takes a village, people!). Thanks go to my critique partner, Jackie Rutherford, who always has insightful feedback, sees things in my stories I've not spotted (and then suddenly appear to be blindingly obvious), and does it all with humor, the right level of compliments, and sharp intelligence.

Thanks to Benita Douglas for teaching me about the hoops people need to jump through to become a doctor. It sounds exhausting to me, and I'm glad Jason gets to join the fully-fledged doctor ranks in the end.

To Amanda Bell who, through a series of frankly hilarious conversations, helped me come up with a bunch of ideas for bad dates. There are more dating shenanigans in the next two books, so thank you so much, Amanda. Thanks to my editor, Karan Eleni of the Letterers Collective, for picking up on all my un-dotted 'i's and uncrossed 't's.

To my family, who put up with a lot when I'm deeply engrossed in my writing. You are my rock, and I'm so, so grateful to you.

And finally, thank you to all my readers. Without you, I couldn't do this. Keep on reading, and I will keep on writing.

About the Author

Kate O'Keeffe is a *USA TODAY* bestselling and award-winning author who writes exactly what she loves to read: laugh-out-loud romantic comedies with swoon-worthy heroes and gorgeous feel-good happily ever afters. She lives and loves in beautiful Hawke's Bay, New Zealand with her family and two scruffy but loveable dogs.

When she's not penning her latest story, Kate can be found hiking up hills (slowly), traveling to different countries around the globe (back when we used to be able to do that), and eating chocolate. A lot of it.

Made in the USA
Middletown, DE
11 December 2021